FIRE BURN

FIRE BURN·

TALES OF WITCHERY

Compiled by Ken Radford

Witches and the Devil riding on broomsticks.

Michael O'Mara Books Limited

First published in Great Britain by
Michael O'Mara Books Ltd
20 Queen Anne Street
London W1N 9FB

British Library Cataloguing in Publication Data

Radford, Ken
 Fire burn.
 I. Title
 823'.914 [F]

ISBN 0-948397-73-X

Editor: Anne Norton
Picture research: Marion Pullen
Design: James Campus

Typeset by Florencetype Ltd, Kewstoke, Avon
Printed and bound in Great Britain by
Redwood Burn Ltd, Trowbridge, Wiltshire.

For all those who died – stripped naked, shaved, shorn.

For all those who screamed in vain to the Great Goddess, only to have their tongues ripped out by the root.

For those who were pricked, racked, broken on the wheel for the sins of their Inquisitors.

For all those whose beauty stirred their torturers to fury; and for those whose ugliness did the same.

For all those who were neither ugly nor beautiful, but only women who would not submit.

For all those quick fingers, broken in the vice.

For all those soft arms, pulled from their sockets.

For all those budding breasts, ripped with hot pincers.

For all those midwives, killed merely for the sin of delivering man to an imperfect world.

For all those witch-women, my sisters, who breathed freer as the flames took them, knowing as they shed their female bodies, the seared flesh falling like fruit in the flames, that death alone would cleanse them of the sin for which they died – the sin of being born a woman who is more than the sum of her parts.

Anonymous 16th century
(Published in E. Jong, *Witches*, New York, 1981)

Contents

Witches and demons feasting at a Sabbat.

Acknowledgements

My thanks are due to the County Archivists and local historians of England, Scotland, Wales and Ireland for their cooperation in reviving tales of long ago; and to the many old folk who searched through their memories for stories which might otherwise be lost forever.

I would also thank all the schoolchildren who have persuaded their great-grandparents to recall tales told them by their forbears.

According to the demonologist Francesco-Maria Guazzo,
witches bound themselves to Satan by a complicated ritual. Some of its
stages are illustrated here by woodcuts from Guazzo's own book.

In a close lane, as I pursued my journey,
    I spy'd a wrinkled hag, with age grown double,
Picking dry sticks and mumbling to herself.
    Her eyes with scalding rheum were gall'd and red.
Cold palsy shook her head, her hands seemed withered,
    And on her crooked shoulders had she wrapt
The tattered remnants of an old striped hanging,
    Which served to keep her carcass from the cold;
So there was nothing of a piece about her.
    Her lower weeds were all o'er coarsely patched
With different coloured rags – black, red, yellow,
    And seem'd to speak variety of wretchedness.

> *The Orphan or Unhappy Marriage*,
> THOMAS OTWAY, Act II

Introduction

In a random survey conducted among a selection of men and women between the ages of eighteen and eighty it was discovered that only a meagre percentage had heard of the Queen of Heaven and the Horned God. Yet in prehistoric times, these were the deities worshipped by people whose customs and beliefs were influenced by superstition. In the distant past, life was far less sophisticated than it is towards the end of the twentieth century.

The Queen of Heaven, or Mother Goddess, represented birth, creation, the harvesting of food and agricultural plenty – all associated with the summer months. The Horned God, with its stag-like antlers, animal skin and cloven hoofs, represented the hunt, the killing for food – activities of the winter.

The Devil instructing witches in the art of making waxen images.

Depending on the time of the year, these were the deities to whom primitive man offered prayers and sacrifices; these were the gods most ancient and enduring to whom he turned with reverence and awe. Life was a constant struggle for survival. When flood or drought ravaged crops it was the Queen of Heaven who had forsaken the sower. When the skies were torn with streaks of lightning and thunder rolled over the hills, it was the anger of the Horned God, wreaking vengeance for earthly misdeeds.

Long after the coming of Christianity these pagan cults lingered on. Mortals worshipped their gods in secret – in hidden groves, in forests or the darkness of caves. As time passed, the Queen of Heaven faded into obscurity, but homage to the Horned God continued. It was this being of animal skin and cloven hoof who became known as Satan or the Devil; and those who chose to worship him were known as witches.

For hundreds of years this cult persisted. But as the Christian faith grew, a dreadful fate befell those who held revel with the Prince of Darkness or dabbled in the art of witchcraft. Between the fourteenth and seventeenth centuries it is recorded that more than half a million people were put to death for practising witchcraft. Most of these were women, for according to the capricious whims of one inquisitor they were more readily caught in the toils of Satan; they were more credulous, more impressionable.

A great number were innocent, falsely accused and then tortured until they confessed. The trials to which they were subjected left little chance of the accused escaping conviction and punishment. Some were bound hand and foot and thrown into a river. If they sank below the surface it was taken as a sign of their innocence, although more often than not they drowned before they were retrieved from the swirling torrent. But should they float, then they were considered the Devil's own, rejected by God's water. Punishment was swift and merciless. The wretched victims were hanged or burnt alive.

Some were weighed against the Holy Bible, and were the scales to tilt it was reasoned that the body was possessed by an earth spirit – a sure indication of witchery. Others were hoisted into the air with heavy stones tied about their feet, there to hang until they confessed or their arms were torn from their sockets. There were thumbscrews, vicious leg breakers and a variety of other cruel

Trial by water. The suspected witch was flung into a pond or stream
with her hands and feet bound together. If she sank she was innocent;
but if she floated she was found guilty of witchcraft and then had
to endure an even more horrible death.

implements of torture. From Germany come tales of the 'Black Virgin', a hinged and hollow iron contraption with spikes that pierced the flesh of those trapped inside.

Stories tell of witches who are beautiful and those who are singularly ugly. Some are as young and attractive as others are old and forbidding, with wizened cheeks, sunken eyes and hair falling grey to the shoulders.

If, in our imagination, we were to journey backward in time, we might come upon a witch of long ago in some moonlit country lane. With her pointed hat and ragged cloak we see her shuffling along, muttering to herself as she makes her way to a sabbat beyond the churchyard walls. Like a shadow a black cat moves behind her, its eyes glowing in the dark. She does not look towards us, for her crooked form keeps her eyes fixed to the ground. And as we pass by we glance over our shoulders, wondering at her second sight and the secrets she hides in her lonely heart.

Mandrake roots were carved and used to cast spells.

Or it might be a girl we come upon – lithe, alluring, her hair shining in the moonlight with the lustre of a raven's wing. Her smile would melt a heart of stone. But who knows what mischief is in her thoughts, and who would not fall under her spell?

Throughout the years there have been countless stories of

witchery, told around the fireside at Hallowe'en or the Eve of
May. Many are lost and will never be heard again. The following
tales, gathered from home and abroad, were found in state and
county archives or lay in the memories of those who recall
characters and incidents related by their forbears.

In the main, the tales reflect the customs and a way of life now
long gone. But some are of recent origin, for although we no
longer hear of screeching hags riding across the sky on broomsticks, there are people who still cling to a belief in witchcraft and
will always remain pagans at heart.

The Wonders of the Invisible World.

OBSERVATIONS

As well *Historical* as *Theological*, upon the NATURE, the NUMBER, and the OPERATIONS of the

DEVILS.

Accompany'd with,

I. Some Accounts of the Grievous Molestations, by DÆMONS and WITCHCRAFTS, which have lately annoy'd the Countrey; and the Trials of some eminent *Malefactors* Executed upon occasion thereof: with several Remarkable *Curiosities* therein occurring.

II. Some Counsils, Directing a due Improvement of the terrible things, lately done, by the Unusual & Amazing Range of EVIL SPIRITS, in Our Neighbourhood: & the methods to prevent the *Wrongs* which those *Evil Angels* may intend against all sorts of people among us. especially in Accusations of the Innocent.

III. Some Conjectures upon the great EVENTS, likely to befall, the WORLD in General, and NEW ENGLAND in Particular; as also upon the Advances of the TIME, when we shall see BETTER DAYES.

IV. A short Narrative of a late Outrage committed by a knot of WITCHES in *Swedeland*, very much Resembling, and so far Explaining, *That* under which our parts of *America* have laboured !

V. THE DEVIL DISCOVERED: In a Brief Discourse upon those TEMPTATIONS, which are the more Ordinary *Devices* of the Wicked One.

By Cotton Mather.

Boston Printed by *Benj. Harris* for *Sam. Phillips.* 1693.

Title page of witch-hunt pamphlet by Cotton Mather.

Witches of Salem

At a time when the state of Massachusetts feared for the spiritual well-being of its community, the younger generation, with lower moral standards than those of its Puritan forbears, threatened to undermine the 'Bible Colony' – to transform it into a haven for heretics.

Drunkenness, profanity and sexual promiscuity were fast increasing. Added to this, as though by some act of divine vengeance, came a disastrous fire in Boston. The colony would perish, believed the elders, unless people reformed their ways.

It was a time when Cotton Mather, a prominent Massachusetts

Witches' Hill, Salem.

clergyman, wrote his account of New England's hauntings and poltergeists, of witches and souls possessed by the Devil. An interest in evil spirits was growing.

More particularly, the fear of witchcraft grew, for it was believed that witches could uncover all secrets, foretell the future, raise ghosts from their tombs. Their victims, by self-induced terror, brought the witches' spells to pass. And once held in the stare of an 'evil eye' they could be released only by the touch of a witch's hand.

In a search for the Devil's disciples, the elderly, eccentric, insane or ill-tempered were all prime suspects. It was a common belief that there was only one way to break a witch's power – to kill her.

Vengeance of Hannah Glover

Towards the end of the seventeenth century a stonemason called John Godwin lived in the village of Salem with his wife and children. They were a happy family, with a pleasant home and comfortable means. Little did they suspect the heartache and anxiety that lay in store.

It all began when the eldest daughter, a spiteful girl with a sharp tongue, accused a maidservant of stealing. 'Each time I look some of my clothes are missing,' she complained angrily as she rummaged through her chest of drawers. 'I shall ask father to send you away!'

Tearfully, the servant protested her innocence; and when no one would believe her she ran from the Godwin home, too distressed to continue with her work.

By comparison, her home was a humble shack where her widowed mother was waiting alone. She was truly roused to anger as she listened to her daughter's story and saw the tears in her eyes.

The widow, Hannah Glover, had little to call her own, and watched over her only child as a vixen guards its cub. Through that day and long after nightfall she sat before her fire, stirring the logs until sparks spat out and flames licked the chimney. As she crouched before the hearth she fashioned a doll of sticks and rags, passing it through the smoke and muttering under her breath. A fearful expression clouded her face, with surly lips and eyes as bright as the sparks in the grate. It was said that even her husband, from the time they were wed until he lay on his deathbed, thought her to be a witch.

In the quiet hours before dawn the Godwin household were awakened as their eldest daughter was stricken with convulsions and cried out from her bed. For a time she was deaf, apart from a distant screech echoing in her ears. Then she was able to utter only a gurgling sound, with her tongue fallen down into her throat.

Before long the other Godwin children were afflicted with a similar seizure, their jaws gaping and then snapping shut, swift and tight as a rat trap. One moment their necks were limp, unable to prevent their heads from falling heavily to their chests, and their tongues hung out at great length upon their chins. A moment later their necks and limbs were rigid, and they whimpered in pain as their backs arched grotesquely.

Their parents were distraught and there was little they could do to ease the children's suffering or discover the cause of it. A doctor was summoned immediately, but being without knowledge of medical science he could diagnose only that his patients had been bewitched.

Prayers were recited by a local clergyman. Then, mercifully, the youngest child recovered and was able to tell of demons that possessed her, and of visions that came in a nightmare – fiery eyes burning in the dark and strange, hoarse mutterings emanating from the corners of her room.

Days passed, and eventually the mystery of the Godwin children's affliction was brought to the attention of Boston magistrates. After a brief investigation Hannah Glover was brought before the court.

The widow was fearless. At her trial she blasphemed and was found unable to recite the Lord's prayer – a sure indication of her being in league with the Devil. 'The Prince of Darkness will watch over me as his own!' she declared defiantly. 'His power breathes within me!'

To display her skills as a disciple of Satan she tightened her fingers around a rag effigy she had about her, whereupon the eldest child of John Godwin stifled a cry and struggled to break free of hands she imagined held fast at her throat.

Hannah Glover's confession and her defiance in the face of all

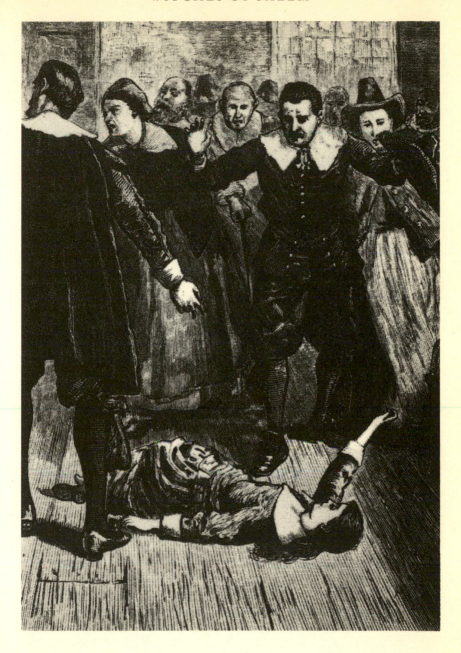

A Salem girl 'possessed' – an engraving made during the witch trials of 1692.

assembled at the court led to a swift verdict by the magistrates. She was condemned as a witch and sentenced to death.

While awaiting execution she was visited in jail by Cotton Mather. 'When I'm gone there will be others to continue the torment,' she told him, unrepentant. It seemed that those who wilfully wronged her only child – her own flesh and blood – were not easily to escape her vengeance.

For a time after her death the strange malady affecting the Godwin children persisted. There were further occasions when they were struck deaf and dumb and plagued with frightful nightmares. Sometimes, convinced that they were able to fly and soar among the clouds, they would race along the ground, flapping their arms like the wings of a bird. But more often their senses were dulled and they would sink into the depths of depression.

If the truth were known, in those days when superstition and fear of the unknown were prevalent, it was the knowledge that the curse of a witch had fallen upon them that made the children frantic with fear. Convulsions, rigid limbs and backward arching of the spine, loss of speech, the delusion of flying – all these would be recognized by a physician of the twentieth century as the symptoms of hysteria.

The Visitor

It happened so long ago that no one will ever know why Susanna Martin sought her revenge on a young man from the village of Salem. Perhaps she was stricken with jealousy or the bitterness of unrequited love. Whatever the reason, her eyes smouldered with hate when he scorned her attentions. And one day when he passed by with not a glance in her direction she stared after him, muttering a curse. 'There'll come a day when some she-devil will steal through the dark to seek him out!' she foretold.

But the young man scorned her with derision, and paid little heed to Susanna's curse. Soon it was forgotten.

Later that summer he was awakened one night by a strange sound. His eyes searched the shadows in his room. The curtains at the window had stirred in the wind, letting in a shaft of moonlight which fell across his bed and crept toward his pillow. Perhaps he had turned in his sleep and it was the light resting on his eyelids that had disturbed him.

With a sigh he pulled the sheet over his face, and soon he was asleep again.

When next he woke, the room was plunged in darkness. In the silence he heard a faint scratching at the window. He threw aside the bedclothes and opened the curtains wide, but there was nothing to be seen. The night was still, with not a breath of wind; and above the rooftops the clouds were edged with silver.

For a while he kept watch, listening for a sound under the eaves or from the street below. It was many minutes before he returned to his bed, resting his head lightly on the pillow so that no further disturbance would escape him. Then, before he had closed his eyes, a scrabbling near the foot of his bed made him sit up with a start.

Beside the wardrobe in the corner two pools of light were glowing, each as small and bright as a candle flame – like the eyes of some creature holding him in its stare. As they drew nearer they shone more brightly. The young man cried out in fright when whatever lurked there sprang at him and with startling agility leapt about the bed, growling and spitting as it tore at his arms while he strove to ward off the attack.

But his struggles were in vain. Moments later he felt sharp claws clutching at his throat. Paralysed with terror, he lay there while the weight of his assailant bore heavily on his chest. In the darkness he could make out only the fiery eyes staring into his, a warm, furry heap pressed upon the length of his body, and a guttural rattle like that of a monstrous cat.

The creature lay upon him for some time; and he sensed that were he to move or cry out its claws would dig deeper into his throat.

At last, in desperation, he muttered, 'In the name of God and all that's holy – Avoid! Avoid!'

As soon as his prayer was uttered, whatever had come to seek him out withdrew its talons, slid to the floor, and passing through the window went off into the night.

Possessed

As time passed, the strange case of Hannah Glover and the Godwin children was almost forgotten. It was four years later, in 1692, when fear once more gripped the inhabitants of Salem.

In the home of the Reverend Samuel Parris lived two young girls, his nine-year-old daughter, Elizabeth, and a younger niece, Abigail. They spent much of their time in the company of a household servant, a West Indian woman known as Tituba. It was she who fascinated the girls with tales of her native land: tales of black magic and the supernatural. Often their eyes were wide with wonder as Tituba foretold the future written in their palms.

Tituba, the Rev. Samuel Parris's servant,
recounting tales of African sorcery to Parris's frightened daughters.

During the long winter evenings the servant's room became the meeting place for Elizabeth and Abigail and many of their young friends who would steal from their homes and gather there in secret. The girls were filled with awe as they listened to stories of ghosts and demons.

The events that followed these clandestine gatherings rekindled the fears that had swept through the village in 1688, for the daughter and niece of Reverend Parris and several other girls of the neighbourhood fell victim to fits of hallucination similar to those which had affected the Godwin children. They woke screaming in the night, and stared at ghosts hovering about the room while their parents tried to comfort them. At other times their bodies writhed, and nothing would console their terror.

'Keep them away!' they would cry, as imaginary spectres lurked in the shadows.

'An evil spirit has possessed them!' the doctors declared. And it was widely believed that the Devil had returned to Salem.

Prayers and chants of exorcism had little effect. Soon the whole community was aroused when the plight of the girls continued. If they were under the spell of witchcraft, the neighbours argued, then there were witches hiding among them.

Time and again the victims were urged to name their tormentors for fear their souls would be lost to the Devil. And so, on the first day of March 1692, three women whose names had been whispered were brought to a local tavern to be questioned by the magistrates. The suspects were Sarah Osburn, a respected citizen who had recently forsaken the church; Sarah Good, a homeless beggar-woman; and Tituba, the servant at the home of Reverend Parris.

For six days the inquisition continued before a crowd of villagers who bore witness to past incidents. 'After a quarrel with Sarah Osburn my cattle lay sick in the byre,' a neighbour remembered. 'It was one evening this winter past,' recalled another, 'Sarah Good came knocking at my door, begging food for her young ones and shelter for the night. We sent her away, with the dogs snapping at her heels. And before dawn the barn burst into flames and our store of grain was burnt.'

'Why do you harm the children?' the accused were asked. 'What contract have you made with the Devil? Confess, or you will be damned for ever!'

Frightened, the women blamed one another, each protesting her own innocence. It was Tituba who at last relented. 'The Devil came to me and bid me make my mark with blood in his book,' she confessed.

As she told her story, some of the girls began to tremble and mutter incoherently to themselves, their eyes staring at someone – something – beyond her.

'Many others had made their mark there,' she continued. 'Sarah Good and Sarah Osburn among them . . .' She went on to describe a spectre of a man in black that had appeared to her. 'His form changed to that of a wolf, standing on its hind legs, its fangs bared. He wanted me for his own, to serve him and bring others into the fold.'

During Tituba's confession many of the bewitched girls present at the hearing were stricken with fits of hysteria, first whimpering, then screaming inconsolably.

'I would never harm the children!' the woman vowed. 'It was the Devil that possessed me!'

On 7th March the three women were committed to gaol. But the hardship and privation of a seventeenth century prison was more than Sarah Osburn could endure. She died there at the beginning of summer.

Despite a day of prayer and fasting at Salem, many girls and young women were still being tormented, and the curse of witchery remained. The villagers were further dismayed when Martha Corey, a devout church member, was accused of harbouring Satan. She could offer no evidence in her defence, and sat in stunned silence throughout the hearing. Asked to describe the appearance of the demons that came to torment her, Ann Putnam, the woman's accuser, replied: 'There was a smell of brimstone, and I heard a sound like the grunting of a hog. But I could not see the Devil or his creatures, for Martha Corey put a spell on me, and for a long time I was blind.'

Further evidence from a clergyman told how the tormented girl rushed about with her arms outstretched as though she imagined she were flying, all the while crying 'Whish . . . whish . . .!' And then she was heard to cry, 'No! I won't! It's the Devil's book!' Sometimes, he recalled, she ran towards the fire and attempted to leap into the flames.

The strange happenings at Salem did not end with the imprisonment of Martha Corey. Before the spring passed, suspicion fell on

**Martha Cory refusing to sign
a confession of witchcraft which led to her being hanged.**

Rebecca Nurse, an elderly God-fearing villager who had never been known to harm a soul. She was brought to the meeting house for examination, and eventually committed to gaol on the most flimsy evidence. At her trial, girls writhed and screamed in torment. 'I see a black man beside her, whispering in her ear!' one cried.

'I am helpless against the mischief of the Devil,' Rebecca protested. 'He can appear in any form – even that of an innocent old lady.'

But despite the apparent suffering of the children – their fears and fits of hysteria – Rebecca Nurse showed no emotion. It was always believed that only witches could shed no tears.

That evening, a sermon delivered in the church roused everyone to anger against the Devil and his evil ways. Fear and mistrust swept through the village. Each day innocent people were accused of witchcraft – farmers, housewives, even a clergyman. All lost their freedom or their lives. It appeared that no one was above suspicion. If malicious storytelling were allowed to continue, observed one sceptic, then everyone would be branded as servants of the Devil.

One piece of evidence was used repeatedly at all the examinations. It was noticed that one glance from the supposed witch brought terror to the victims – a terror that was calmed only by the touch of the accused's hand.

And so the witch hunt spread beyond Salem. From bitter experience it was learned that the surest way to avoid suspicion was to accuse another. More and more were crying 'Witch!' and pointing a finger at a neighbour. It was also realized that to escape execution one had only to confess. It was those who stubbornly denied their accusers who were carted off to Gallows Hill, after endless inquisition, pleading by friends and relatives, and sometimes torture by the law officers.

One prisoner, convinced of the injustice and terrible wrong inflicted on himself and fellow villagers, and sickened by the lies and torture, appealed to an eminent New England clergyman for the trials to be taken away from the prejudice prevalent at Salem, and to be held instead in Boston.

Gradually, the witchcraft panic subsided. There were murmurs of protest, and sympathy for the victims from among the crowds that gathered on Gallows Hill.

It is said that it was the courage of one man that made a lasting impression of the villagers. A more terrible fate than that suffered by his wife, Martha, befell Giles Corey. Arrested on the same charge of harbouring the Devil, he chose neither to confess nor to denounce his accusers. Instead, he maintained a dignified silence throughout his trial, refusing to answer the magistrates' questions. For his defiance of the court he received the punishment prescribed by their laws. Stretched on the ground with his arms and legs pinioned, he had weights piled upon him in ever increasing numbers, until he was forced to obey the court's ruling or else be crushed. For two days Giles Corey endured this torture. His suffering and death did much to influence public opinion.

By the spring of 1693 most prisoners held on a charge of practising witchcraft had had their sentences suspended. But many were to remain in gaol or live out their lives in poverty, for before their release they were required to pay for the cost of their imprisonment – even the cost of forging the iron chains that bound them.

As the years passed, a number of families who lived at Salem left the village, never to return. Gone, too, were the hysterical outbursts of the girls. The witchcraft phenomenon was looked upon as a strange fever, induced by fear and vivid imagining. The 14th January, 1697, was set aside in Massachusetts as a day for fasting and prayer – a day for the people to ask God's forgiveness for what had happened five years ago.

Of all the girls whose irresponsible actions had brought misery to others, only one – Ann Putnam – expressed remorse for her misdeeds. In 1706, now a young woman, she asked to be accepted back into the church. With her head bowed she stood before the congregation while the minister read her admission from the pulpit. In her statement she repented that as a child she had brought about the downfall of others, '. . . And I can truly say before God that I did it not out of anger or ill-will, but ignorantly, while I was under the spell of Satan . . .'

How will the witchcraft delusion at Salem be remembered?

Some historians claim that it was a vengeful plot, deliberately contrived by the girls of the village, with the knowledge and the encouragement of certain adults: a vengeance born of spite and jealousy. Others say that it grew out of all proportion as a result of mass hysteria. Perhaps it was a combination of both, kindled by the imagination of impressionable girls, caught in a train of events beyond their control.

Whatever the truth may be, who could have foreseen that before the winter of 1692 twenty people would die on the gallows, a hundred and fifty be imprisoned, and countless others flee the colony?

It is believed that events at Salem marked the beginning of the end of witchcraft trials in England and Europe.

The Devil's Own

It is recorded that during the reign of Henry VII 'in the year of our Lord fourteen hundred eighty and six', there lived in the village of Knaresborough among the Yorkshire moors an orphaned girl who was barely sixteen years old. She is remembered as Agatha Southeil.

Come wind or rain her clothes were scant and torn, clinging about her shapely limbs and firm figure. Her hair was as black as a raven's wing, falling over her shoulders and shading her eyes that glittered in the light of the moon and sun.

Agatha was a dreamer who roamed among the whins and fells, with nothing but paltry relief from the parish and the food she begged to keep her from starvation and a pauper's grave.

The Devil disguised as a handsome young man.
Only his clawed feet reveal him as not being human.

34

One evening, as she wandered beyond her shack on the moors, she came upon a stranger who was dressed in the cloak and hat as worn by a gentleman. She had not noticed him approach along the path, perhaps because her eyes were lowered as she sat for a while upon a rock weeping quietly, wondering whether once more she would go hungry to her bed.

Seeing her alone and troubled, the stranger came close. Why should one so young and attractive be sad, he wondered. He bent down, brushing a tear from her cheek. His touch was as cold as a churchyard tomb. And when she looked up with a start his eyes held her spellbound in their fiery gaze. She was not to know that it was the Prince of Darkness, the Devil himself, who hid behind the guise of a handsome young man.

He drew closer still, putting his arms about her shoulders to comfort her. And feeling her tremble his eyes burned brighter.

'Why so sad, my pretty one?' asked he.

She told him how she was alone and hungry. Good fortune had passed her by, and there was never a word of kindness wherever she roamed. Doors were slammed in her face. Sometimes the villagers set their dogs to snarl and snap at her heels.

'Dry your tears,' said the stranger, and promised that if she were to put her trust in him her fortune would change. There would be no more poverty and despair, and riches would be her reward.

For a long time he stayed with her, until dusk crept over the moors. Agatha was charmed by the Devil's wiles and fell further under his spell. No one had shown her such sympathy. Not since her mother was dead had she known compassion. She looked up at the darkening sky. And then, strange to say, when she turned again to her companion he had vanished as mysteriously as he had appeared. She was alone with the whins and the moonlight.

That night she lay awake, wondering whether it had all been an hallucination – whether she had fallen asleep on the moors and the stranger had come to her in a dream. But when the first light of dawn showed at her window her hopes were rekindled, for about her shack she found coins of copper and gold, lying on her pillow and strewn around the bare floor.

In the days that followed, the Devil came many times to visit Agatha, always in the guise of a young gentleman with a winsome smile and somniferous eyes. His charm and charisma won her

The Devil carrying a witch off to Hell from
Historia de Gentibus Septentrionalibus, by Olaus Magnus, Rome, 1555.

affection, and presently he became her first love, arousing unknown passion in her heart. Once he came to her miserable
dwelling and carried her off on a stallion as black and swift as a
storm cloud. Far away they rode, over hills and dales with a
thundering of hoofs and the rushing of wind, until a magnificent
house came in sight, its windows all aglow. Servants prepared a
feast for their master and his guest. There was wine and music and
splendour such as Agatha had never imagined. The world lay at her
feet, she was promised, now that she was the Devil's lover. Only
he could ransack earth's treasures, stir thunder and lightning, and
lavish upon her powers beyond her dreams, with which she could
trouble and maim whomever she pleased, plague young and old
with fearful nightmares and unveil what lay in the future as readily
as she remembered events of the past.

When the feasting was over and Agatha's thoughts reeled with
wine and promises of fortune to come, the lamps were dimmed. At
the Devil's invitation she recited the words of some strange
incantation. Whereupon the vaulted roof of heaven swirled and
rumbled. The house and all around her vanished as she seemed to
tumble through a pool of darkness until she awakened, bewildered,

to find herself wandering the moors in the moonlight near her shack.

Thereafter, a wild glint showed in Agatha's eyes. Her face was pale and drawn, with none of the freshness of her youth.

'Some mischief has befallen her!' villagers muttered one with another.

'Her eyes burn, and her flesh is wasting away like an unwrapped mummy!'

'I'm thinking some hag has rid her!'

The spellbound girl scorned their pity and taunted them with fistfuls of coins she snatched from her pocket. But in her hand she clutched only withered heather and aspen leaves.

As though in a trance, she usually slept through the day, rising from her bed at nightfall to hold revel with the Prince of Darkness and other of his disciples in the marshes beyond the cemetery wall. So still did she lie, wearing a fearful grimace, that villagers who peered through her window wondered if she were dead. And once, when awakened, she began to dance about the room to the strains of some haunting music, oblivious of those who stared in wonder.

'The lass is truly bewitched!' they gasped, backing away in fright. Then a sudden gust of wind sent the women's skirts billowing over their thighs.

Stories are remembered of horned goats appearing in the vicinity of Agatha Southeil's hovel, carrying on their backs naked, flesh-shrivelled hags who screeched with laughter. From neighbouring villages folk journeyed to Knaresborough to see for themselves the girl said to be possessed of the Devil. But Agatha took vengeance on all who came to taunt her. Some were stricken with fever, others with deformity. When a farmer's plough horse writhed in the throes of death, the beast's stomach was found to contain not hay and oats but fish-hooks and thorns of thistle.

Accounts of the young witch's mischief were brought to the attention of the Justices who dispatched their stoutest bailiffs to apprehend her. Undaunted by the squawking of crows and the hissing of serpents that stood vigil at the door, they went inside and dragged her away.

During her inquisition and medical examination it was discover-ed that Agatha was with child. But the father of her baby was no mortal whit, she protested. He was a prince whose mastery knew no bounds, who held dominion over man and beast and breathed fear into their hearts.

Concluding that she was just an ignorant wench, mentally and emotionally unstable and easily seduced, the Justices paid no attention to such hysterical rambling and set her free – a compassionate verdict at a time when heresy was so cruelly punished.

But the villagers were less indulgent, continuing to persecute the girl mercilessly. Tormented by dogs and stones and bitter tongues she was at last driven from her shack and forced to seek shelter on the moors.

The span of forty weeks expired, and the birth of her child spelled the end of Agatha Southeil's miserable life, barely had she reached the age of seventeen. It is said that her death was attended by a howling wind which drowned the screams that echoed in the cavern where she lay.

Close to her body they discovered a newborn female of grotesque shape. Its head was disproportionately large, with goggling eyes that burned like fire. Its cheeks were shrunken, and the mouth bore a clearly defined impression of teeth, with the upper canines protruding like the tusks of a young wild boar. Misshapen limbs joined the body as though screwed together piece by piece. Those who found the child turned their eyes in revulsion.

With no mother to watch over it, the foundling became a ward of the parish and was placed in the care of a kindly woman who gave it the name Ursula.

A stranger child she had never known. It ate greedily and slept for only a few hours each day, lying awake through the night to stare into the darkness. She told how, sometimes when the night was calm, curtains stirred, doors slammed, and shutters swung wildly on the hinges. Once, when the infant was left lying in its crib, the woman returned to find her home ransacked. Windows were shattered, burning embers were strewn in the hearth, furniture was broken and upturned. Distressed, she ran to her neighbours who were afraid to cross the threshold, repelled by a fierce hissing and wailing as though wild cats were crouching behind the door waiting to spring at them.

Anxious for the safety of the child, the foster mother ventured inside. But the infant Ursula was nowhere to be seen. 'Some evil goblin has spirited the baby away!' she cried.

Every nook and cranny was searched, until the infant and crib were found wedged in the chimney.

As Ursula grew, so did her deformity and unnatural temper. She bitterly resented reproach and bared her teeth menacingly whenever she was chastized. It seemed that never a day went by when she was not attended by her father, the Devil, who lurked about the home of her guardian, appearing sometimes as a large dog with baleful eyes; other times making his presence felt with a cacophony of weird sounds and fearful happenings. The walls and floor would tremble and pulsate like heartbeats growing louder. The food on their plates would turn to mould. Crockery was flung about the room as though by a raging poltergeist. Invisible hands clawed and scratched at the foster mother, tearing her clothes from her back and laying icy fingers upon her flesh.

But always the bedevilled Ursula would only chuckle. 'Why,' she would say, 'don't be fright. There's nowt here to harm you and me.'

The foster mother was a simple, God-fearing soul, who lived in fear of the unknown. In despair she pleaded with the parish to take the child away, and at length her appeals were answered. It was then that Ursula was taken into their care, and being now of age, she was put to school where she might be taught to read and write.

The schoolmistress wondered at the imagination and speed of learning of a child blessed with none of the naivety and affection of her sex and tender years. Jealous of her scholarly success, other pupils mocked Ursula's misshapen appearance, but none escaped her vengeance. The tormentors were pinched or burned and stripped of their clothing when no one was near. At times they were struck dumb for an hour or more, their lips and tongues swollen by some mysterious affliction.

As their schooldays passed, children learned to fear the young witch who could summon demons and plague them with nightmares. Parents grew angry when they were told of her spite and wickedness. And so it came about that she was excluded from the school and from the care of the parish, and left to fend for herself, with neither kin nor home she could call her own.

The years wore on. Now a young woman, Ursula earned the reputation of a soothsayer with remarkable understanding and foresight. Although she uttered her prophesies in strange riddles, people came from near and far to consult the Knowing One of Knaresborough. The old asked that she spell some word of the hereafter; the young wondered whether their love was true and what fortune was hidden in the future.

It is recorded that in the year 1512 Ursula married a man called Toby Shipton, although history remembers nothing of him. Thereafter, she was known as Mother Shipton and her reputation spread to distant counties. She was revered as a fortune teller and, by virtue of her forbidding appearance, feared as a witch.

Mother Shipton

A chronicle of prophesies is attributed to Mother Shipton. It is said that with uncanny accuracy she foretold the end of Cardinal Wolsey; the deaths and accessions of kings and queens of England; wars and historic events during their reigns. In those days of primitive transportation, she foresaw a time 'when carriages without horses run . . .' and when sailing craft were at the mercy of the seas it was written:

Iron in the water shall float
As easily as a wooden boat.

When education was reserved for the privileged few, and common folk lived their lives in ignorance, Mother Shipton's vision shone into the invisible:

All England's sons that plough the land
Shall be seen with book in hand.
Learning shall so ebb and flow;
The poor shall more wisdom know.

Who but she could have forewarned that during the seventeenth century London would be stricken with plague and ravaged by flames. Pepys' diary of October 1666, describing the great fire of London, records that 'Shipton's prophesy is out':

Triumphant death rides London through,
And men on top of houses go . . .

It is as well for our forbears that some events were clouded in her crystal ball, for once she wrote:

This world to an end shall come
In eighteen hundred and eighty-one.

History books are silent regarding the life of Mother Shipton, but the whispers of local legend have much to relate. It is likely that some stories are imagined, since we are told that she was born in 1486, while other accounts tell of her death in 1651! Yet it is commonly believed that long ago, near the Dropping Well at Knaresborough, there lived a sibyl remembered as a witch and fortune teller.

Unlike other heretics of the fifteenth and sixteenth centuries, Mother Shipton did not end her days on the gallows. She foretold the time of her death, and when the day came she lay on her bed awaiting the call of the ferryman. Her life span was 'three score and thirteen years'. A poet of that age wrote an epitaph for her grave:

Here lies she who never ly'd,
Whose skill so often hath been try'd.
Her prophesies shall still survive,
And ever keep her name alive.

Old Nan's Ghost

Her hair was coarse and black, falling in coils from the brim of a pointed hat to hang about her shoulders. Her lips were tightly pursed, hidden among the furrows of her cheeks. Come summer or winter she was wrapped in a shawl that trailed almost to the ground, its edges clutched at her throat.

Villagers crossed to the other side of the street whenever she approached, afraid that her sharp eyes would hold them in her stare. Some threw coppers at her feet, more from fear than compassion. They knew that she would curse those who incurred her displeasure. From door to door she shuffled along, begging and stealing or seeking shelter when the night was cold. 'Just a bundle of straw in the barn to lay my weary bones on,' she would say.

But there came a time when no one could drive her off, nor fear her vengeance. Two summers since, Old Nan had succumbed to hunger and exposure, and it is likely that her bones lay scattered somewhere in a cave. They say that her ghost still haunts the hills and moors of Yorkshire.

One night a tinker was trundling along the road from North-allerton to Stokesley. The lantern which hung from his horse-drawn cart was swaying to and fro, throwing pools of light upon the ground. Then, from out of the darkness, a figure appeared in his path.

It was an old woman who stood there, her arm raised above her head. The horse reared and whinneyed restively.

'Who's there?' the tinker called, peering forward.

No one answered. Instead, the woman took the bridle and led the horse along a rough track which branched off from the road. Over ruts and stones the cart rattled and lurched. Although the tinker tugged at the reins the horse plodded on relentlessly. With a curse he leapt from his seat and cracked his whip to drive off the woman who led him astray. But he might as well have clutched at shadows, for the hunched figure that held the bridle moved on, unhindered, and the mesmerized horse followed.

Farther on they came to a halt where the path petered out beneath the shoulder of a hill. Here the old woman pointed to the entrance of a cavern, concealed by fronds of bracken. As though he were under her spell, the tinker moved closer at her beckoning, unhitching the lantern from his cart. He ventured inside, his light searching the corners.

In a cleft above his head he found a draw-string pouch of flannel, heavy with silver charms and golden rings and a handful of sovereigns. It was Old Nan's treasure that was hidden there, hoarded through years of begging and stealing, and now glistening in the light of the lantern.

A voice echoed in the cavern, 'It's for her . . . for her,' the ghost of Old Nan was heard to say.

Had it not been for the coins and jewellery now glittering in his hand, the tinker would have trembled with fear. Instead, his eyes shone with greed at his new-found fortune.

The voice of Old Nan echoed on. She told of a long-lost grandchild who wandered somewhere over the moors, and sighed when she thought of her poverty and loneliness. The treasure was for the old woman's loved one, to buy fine clothes and happiness. And it was the tinker she had chosen to seek her out. Five sovereigns he should keep for himself, for fulfilling a kindly mission.

'Search the moors until you find her . . . find her. Or beware . . . beware!' were the ghost's last words, as she left the entrance and was swallowed up in the night.

As the years passed, the tinker prospered and became a wealthy merchant of Stokesley. He had forgotten the waif who wandered the moors, and the pouch of gold and silver he kept for himself with never a pang of conscience.

There were times when, in his dreams, he would return to that hidden cavern, and awaken with a start to hear again Old Nan's warning transcending the years. But he would turn over and fall asleep again, for now the old witch was dead and gone – just an echo from the past.

Then one evening the merchant was riding home from the market at Northallerton. Dusk was falling as he passed a rough track leading off the road. Something startled his horse and spurred it to a gallop, fleeing in terror as if from some fearful presence. It approached the village of Stokesley at a furious pace while the merchant cried out in alarm, lashing with his whip at something that seized him from behind.

The Devil presenting a witch with a familiar in the form of a black dog. Familiars were supernatural spirits often assuming animal forms who attended and aided witches and wizards.

According to a farmer they passed on the road, the rider was struggling to escape the clutches of someone clinging to his shoulders. 'I would swear it was a woman,' the farmer went on, lowering his voice to a whisper. 'She was an old crone with a long shawl wrapped about her, wearing a pointed hat with a wide brim. And her hair was blowing wild in the wind!'

When the runaway horse reached the village it was frothing at the mouth and panting with exhaustion. And the merchant's corpse lay slouched over the saddle, his legs tangled in the stirrups.

Simmer Water

It was early one morning when a gipsy woman came to Simmer-dale from the moors. Her basket was filled with sprigs of heather and posies of wild flowers tied together with reeds.

Her only company was that of a mongrel who padded along at her side, growling at anyone who came too close or called unkindly from across the street.

First she passed through the churchyard where she laid some flowers on a grave. Who she remembered no one knew, and it is likely that no one cared. Lowering her head, she lingered there a while. Then she hitched up her skirts and wandered on along the cobbled street.

From cottage to cottage she made her way, knocking upon the doors with her stick. 'A sprig of heather to bring good luck? Fresh flowers to sweeten the parlour?'

But many doors were slammed in her face when it was found that a gipsy stood at the threshold. And some would have driven her to the garden gate had not her mongrel bared its teeth.

Undaunted, she climbed the cobbled hill. Yet wherever she called there was no charity and never a word of kindness. As the morning wore on she grew weary and sad.

When the sun was high she came to the crown of the hill where the last cottage in the village stood. It was the home of a Quaker woman who lived alone. The windows were open to let in the summer breeze, and ivy coated the walls.

The gipsy opened the gate and walked up the path beneath an arch of roses.

'A sprig of heather to bring good luck . . .' she began when the door was opened. And she was surprised to be welcomed with a friendly smile.

'Come in and rest a while,' the Quaker woman said. 'It's a long climb up the hill, and you look so hot and tired.'

Witches would often approach grave diggers
and beg for teeth and bones to bury in clay images.

She took the basket and helped the old gipsy over the step. Then she sat her down at the table and brought from the larder what little food she had to share with her visitor. There was bread and cheese, a cool glass of homemade ginger beer, and meat scraps for the dog.

When they had eaten and chatted for a time, the Quaker woman chose a posy of wild flowers and put them in a jar of water. Then she squeezed several coppers into the gipsy's hand, and stroked the mongrel's coat. 'There would be more if it were mine to give. God bless you and speed you on your way.'

Before she passed over the shoulder of the hill, the gipsy turned to look back upon the village, remembering the harsh words and bitterness she had encountered at each doorstep.

Waving her ash stick, she muttered a curse on all who had treated her unkindly. She stared down into the valley and then up into the sky. 'Simmerdale . . . Simmerdale . . . sink forever!' she called.

Throughout that autumn and winter the heavens were plunged in darkness, hiding the sun by day and the moon at night. Torrential rains swelled the streams and rivers until the water lay deep in the valley. Relentlessly it crept higher, covering the church and the villagers' homes. The floods were never to subside. Simmerdale was gone forever, with only a solitary cottage at the top of the hill where its fingers did not reach.

And now, in its place, stands Simmer Water, a peaceful lake near Askrig in the North Riding of Yorkshire. Those who live in the area say that if you peer into its depths when the sun is bright you can make out the shape of the church and the cottages of the village shimmering beneath. And stories are told of a posy of wild flowers whose colours never fade which are sometimes seen floating on the surface.

Witch of the Whins

Some stories of the early nineteenth century portray Nan Hardwick as old and gaunt, her hair grey and unkempt. Other tales recall Nan as an orphan, her eyes as deep as the night sky holding many a young man under her spell. The old clothes she wore hid her shapely thighs and firm breasts, but none who pursued her could win her affection.

For a long time it was wondered whether she was an old woman, hunched in a dark cape, past caring about the curious glances of those she met; or whether it was a young heart that beat within her. It is now so long ago that there is no one to remember. Perhaps, with the passing years, memories of a vivacious girl who set men's hearts pounding, and a woman grown old and bitter, have been confused and left to the imagination of those who recall the tales of long ago.

Some believe they lived together – an old woman and granddaughter. Others say that with her wiles and witchery she chose to be whatever age she fancied: that sometimes she roamed the moors with weary steps and shoulders drooped, and then lay down to sleep with the dreams and longings of a young girl.

Whether she was in the flower of youth or past her three-score years and ten, it is recorded that Nan Hardwick lived alone in an old stone cottage near the river which flowed through the Yorkshire dales. And every evening it was her custom to squat among the whins on the water's edge and gaze towards the sunset.

It had been a tiring day, wandering the dales, begging for a bite to eat at the scattered farmhouses. Home at last, she rested at her favourite place, where the river murmured and the evening breeze was cool. She did not look around when some rowdy men from the village passed by.

'It's auld Nan Hardwick, waiting for the Devil to come along,' taunted the ring-leader. 'Searching the horizon for her long lost child-hood!' laughed another. 'Snaggle-toothed hag! Witch!' they called.

Insults and stones they hurled at her, but none found its mark. Her face turned towards the sunset, and they saw only her crooked back and grey hair hanging down.

When their tormenting was over, the young men drifted off, threatening that before long they would be back to seek her out. 'The hounds will find her and drive her from the parish!' one of them called over his shoulder.

Dusk had fallen the following day. As always, Auld Nan was sitting among the whins when she heard the baying of hounds growing louder. She was afraid that once they had found the scent they would pursue her relentlessly. So she rose from her resting place and ran off through the heather. With surprising haste and agility she made for her cottage and bolted the door behind her. There she hid in the shadows while the sound of her pursuers drew near.

Soon their voices were heard outside. 'You can't escape, old woman! Now weave your spells and borrow the swiftness of a hare. There's nowhere to run and hide with the hounds to track you down!'

They beat upon the door so furiously that the bolt and timbers rattled. The hounds barked with excitement, scratching to find a way in.

'Leave me in peace!' she cried, more in fear than anger. But they laughed at her pleading, and kindled a fire against the door.

'There's nothing can save you, old hag! The dogs have found your scent!'

Smoke billowed in and flames licked the timbers. Before long, while Auld Nan trembled in the corner of her cottage, the doorway was ablaze. In desperation she burst through the flames and ran out into the gathering darkness.

The hounds were released and pursued her in full cry. Swift as a deer she fled, darting in all directions through the gorse and broom and heather, always confounding the beasts that yelped at her heels. Sometimes she would vanish before their eyes, only to reappear elsewhere.

Her tormentors stared in wonder, unable to believe the speed and agility with which she dodged and weaved. 'My God! Do you see that!' one cried, as he watched a lithe figure leap about and heard her youthful scream. 'The old witch has lost her crooked back and runs with the vigour of a girl!'

One moment she flew close to her tormentors, her eyes burning with hate. The next she appeared farther away, as though a streak of light had flashed past them. Incessantly the hounds gave chase, baring their fangs at a phantom prey.

When, at last, they came skulking back and lay panting on the ground, there was neither girl nor old woman to be seen. By guile and witchery Nan Hardwick had escaped.

In vain, the hounds later searched for her scent. The ruffians forced their way beyond the smouldering threshold where they rummaged through the cottage and kicked Auld Nan's mean possessions all about. Night had fallen when they wandered off across the moor.

Winter had set in before they caught sight of the old woman again. They came upon her when they were on their way from a tavern in the village of Castleton.

It was on the bridge which spanned a river at Danby Dale where they met. Remembering her cunning, and afraid of her powers beyond their understanding, they were tempted to turn about. But her shuffling step and her head hung low made them bold. The bridge was narrow, with barely enough room for one to cross at a time. So they barred her way, the leader clutching the hemmel (handrail) on either side.

'Back, old woman!' he commanded, threatening to throw her into the river if she did not give way.

Auld Nan raised her eyes, but did not speak. There followed a murmuring and a muttering, and then a sudden wind whined through the dale. It came nearer, howling now and growing in intensity, seizing her assailants in its icy grip. They hung on, clutching at the hemmel. But the winter squall was fierce, unceasing. It snatched away their breath and held them fast until their bones were frozen to the marrow. For a minute or more it prevailed; and when it died away they were left petrified where they stood, unable to stir a limb or utter a cry.

Auld Nan shuffled on across the bridge. Too numbed to feel its touch, they had the sensation of her body passing through them, as though nothing had stood in her path.

It was morning before the young men were found lying in the river bed, dazed and shivering with cold and fright. When the spell had released its hold on them they had toppled over the hemmel into the water below. And there they would surely have drowned had it not been for the autumn drought.

＊　　＊　　＊

One evening two young farmers were returning from the fields when they came upon a girl who was gathering wild flowers beside the causey, an ancient horse road leading to the village of Oenthorpe.

She wore only a ragged frock, with a sprig of heather in her hair. Her eyes were lowered shyly when they called to her.

'Have you lost your way, lass – all alone here on the moor?'

She backed away as they approached.

'Don't be afraid. There's no one to harm you.'

They came towards her, one from either side, as though they were stalking a wild pony ready to break away. Soon they were beside her, watching with amusement the spark of fear in her eyes as she glanced from one to the other.

'Why do you tremble? We will help you find your way,' they teased. 'You never know who you might meet, now that dusk is falling.'

The young men came closer still, one reaching out to hold the girl's hand while the other seized her from behind. He felt her breasts heave as her breathing deepened and she struggled to break free. Her frock was torn and her thighs laid bare as she wrestled on the ground, whimpering with fright. Then she lay still as they released their hold to watch her sob and tremble. Stark fear gave her strength as she kicked wildly and fought to escape. Startled, they fell back as she leapt to her feet and fled. Farther and faster she ran, her heart pounding as she flew through the whins and heather. But whenever she glanced around, her pursuers were never far behind.

'You can't run for ever. There's nowhere to hide on the moor,' they taunted.

But she was strong and nimble, and terror quickened her flight.

Gradually the distance between them stretched wider. They watched her make straight for a cottage beyond the whins, scurry inside and shut the door behind her.

When her assailants reached her hiding place they listened for some sound from within, prowling around, peeping at the window. They could see smoke curling from the chimney, but the cottage was silent.

'Anyone there?' they called at length, knocking on the door.

No one answered. They imagined the girl hiding inside, hoping they had lost sight of her, longing to hear their footsteps grow faint.

Witches disturbed escape on broomsticks up the chimney.

They tried the latch, but a bolt held the door fast. 'Anyone there?' they called again.

Presently they heard the bolt rattle, and the door was held open wide enough for an old woman with sharp eyes and grey hair to peer out at them.

'Well now, who is this come to call on Auld Nan so late in the day? Two handsome young men, I'm thinking.' She opened the door wider, letting in the last of the daylight. 'Come, rest a spell and tell me what brings you visiting a lonely soul all the way across the moor.'

They looked beyond her into the heavy shadows as they crossed the threshold. The curtains at the window were closed, and there was a glow from the hearth.

'A dark-haired lass has lost her way,' the visitors began. 'Now she's nowhere to be found. Perhaps she called here for shelter.'

Their eyes wandered around the room, expecting to find someone hiding in the corner. Beside the fireplace stood a rocking chair draped with a blanket. Beyond lay a crumpled heap which served as the old woman's bed. Perhaps the clothes would stir and a frightened girl would appear. The rest of the room was hidden in darkness.

Auld Nan chuckled to herself. 'A dark-haired lass, you say? Lost among the whins? Whoever would be wandering so far from home when night is creeping on?'

She took one last peep outside, closed the door and shuffled to her chair. 'Come to the fire and rest a spell. There's a cold wind stirring.'

She poked at the logs until the flames danced and lit up her face. 'I wonder what the young maid could be doing, all alone on the moor,' she went on muttering to herself. 'Could be a ghost you are seeking.'

Bewildered, the visitors strayed from the hearth and looked more closely into the shadows. But where the girl had gone remained a mystery.

'No one ever calls on Auld Nan,' the old woman went on. 'Not for many seasons past. It makes me glad to have a bit of company. And bless by soul, such handsome visitors too. Come, warm yourselves around the fire before you go on your way.'

As they all sat in the firelight she poked at the logs again, her eyes bright with excitement. She looked from one to the other. 'My old grannie use to say that if you gaze long and hard into the grate the smoke and flames will draw a picture of your fortune. I'm thinking you might find visions of your lost maid there.' She saw their eyes searching around. 'You'll not find her hiding in the corner. There's not a soul could steal over the threshold and escape Auld Nan's sharp eyes.'

Each moment the fire burned more fiercely and clouds of smoke drifted to the rafters. While Auld Nan rocked contentedly backwards and forwards in her chair, her visitors wanted to draw back from the heat of the flames which leapt up the chimney. Mysteriously, they found that they were unable to move, as though some power held them fast.

'Watch! Watch the flames! The pictures are getting clear!' they heard the old woman chuckle. But the smoke burned their eyes and throats, and their arms were raised to ward off the intense heat. Gasping for breath, they could utter only strangled cries.

For many minutes the spell held them captive, and the old woman's chuckles grew to a screech of laughter to see their clothes scorch and their hair singe.

When, at last, she set them free, their faces were blistered and they stumbled blindly, groping for the door. They found the latch and staggered outside, gasping the cool air of the moor. The old woman followed to the door, calling after them. 'Come again if you're passing by. Auld Nan is always pleased to have some company. And should I come upon that dark-haired lass I'll tell her you were kind enough to call.'

Aud Mally

Aud Mally – as she was called – lived alone in a derelict farmhouse not far from the village of Guisborough in North Yorkshire. The windows she had boarded up with pieces of timber and part of the roof was open to the sky.

In Teeside she was remembered as a surly, shriven-faced woman who begged for coppers in the villages thereabout. To keep her from a pauper's grave she stole fowl from the local farmers and scratched turnips from their fields. Teeth were scattered in her gums like tombstones in a moonlit churchyard. Her eyes were dark and sunken, as caverns in a barren hillside; and her hair was always tucked beneath her collar and clung about her ears.

One summer day Aud Mally dared to knock at the door of a prosperous farmer who had cattle galore and land that stretched as far as the horizon. 'A crust o' bread and a pocket of taters for a hungry soul,' she begged, keeping her voice soft and her eyes fixed to the ground.

But the farmer had a fiery temper and a heart of stone. 'Clear off!' he said, brandishing his stick. 'Ahv nowt for beggars!' And he followed her to the gate, shouting angrily as she shuffled away, muttering to herself. Perhaps he had never heard tales of the witch-woman's spells, or chose not to believe them.

Before many days had passed, the farmer was troubled when he found that his cows – the finest in the county – were yielding no milk. A fever had come upon them, he feared, or a thief was prowling after dark. So he set one of his field hands to keep watch through the night.

His vigil was in vain, for during the hours of darkness nothing stirred in the meadow where the cows were kept. However, at first light the beasts' udders hung limp, although they lowed and grazed and swished their tails, with no sign of sickness about them.

The field hand lay in wait the next night, and many nights

A witch feeding her familiars.

afterwards. But even though he snatched no more than a few hours' sleep he heard only an owl crying out to the moon and the distant bark of a fox. And every morning when the cocks crowed, the cows were drained of milk.

The summer wore on and the mystery remained. So one night the farmer decided to keep watch himself.

As darkness fell he crouched among the trees beside the meadow, his eyes searching the hedges, his shotgun at the ready. He determined that however stealthily the thief approached, he would never escape unnoticed.

Midnight approached. The lamp burning in the farmhouse went out as the household retired to bed. For a long time the moon was hidden behind the clouds. In the darkness and silence he became a little afraid. Overhead, leaves whispered in the breeze, and silhouettes showed black against the sky.

The hours passed slowly as he waited there peering ino the night. He turned up the collar of his coat, and many times he was tempted to give up his vigil and go to the comfort of his bed. But with true northern grit he stuck to his task. No thief would get the better of him.

In the darkest hours before the dawn the moon reappeared,

56

spreading its ghostly light across the meadow. The cows looked quite contented, some with their heads lowered, tearing at the clover. Others were huddled against the hedges.

Another hour passed. It was then that the farmer began to wonder whether the dusky light was playing tricks with his eyes, or whether something stirred in the corner of the meadow. He was alert now, staring into the moonlight, groping for his shotgun. There were only clumps of bullrushes growing beside the stream and swaying gently from side to side . . . But there it was again! Something was moving among them – darting forward and then crouching low.

As he watched, a flurry of clouds swept across the moon, one moment plunging the meadow into darkness, and then allowing the light to filter through. Whatever he had seen among the rushes was approaching, and seemed to be growing larger each time it came into view. It was more animal than human, for now he could make out the drooping ears, and forelegs raised to its chest. If it were not standing more than five feet tall he would have thought it to be a hare, but he could not imagine a hare of such proportion, unless it happened to be a creature heard of only in folk tales.

With thoughts in confusion and imagination set alight, he began to recall stories which told of witches' familiars, sent at their bidding on errands of mischief. Safe in her hovel, the witch would hang a rope over a beam and tug at it in the pretence of milking a cow. Then her familiar – a spirit conjured by sorcery – would be sent to the meadow or byre to discharge her evil whim.

The farmer shuddered at the thought of it.

Closer came the creature, passing the cattle and making its way toward his hiding place. In desperation he fired his gun; but the shot went astray, and the familiar came on.

Now it was almost upon him. Trembling with fright, he could see that it was not an animal with furry coat and drooping ears. Before him stood a woman with sunken eyes and withered cheeks, her hair tucked under her collar and clinging about her ears.

The farmer let out a cry of terror and fled from the meadow. Over hedge and ditch he stumbled, not once looking back until he reached the farmhouse door.

Until the dawn he lay trembling in his bed, never daring to peep from the window. And when morning came he stuffed some bread and freshly picked vegetables into a sack. Then he sent a farm-boy on an errand to a deserted house near the village of Guisborough where Aud Mally the beggar-woman lived.

Aud Mally.

Book of Shadows

A cover of cloth or coarse-hewn leather covered the parchment leaves upon which secrets were scrawled over the years by those described as Knowing Ones of long ago. Therein were revealed the mysteries of witchcraft – spells and incantations, strange recipes to cure and induce love and heartache: 'marigold petals in a wood fire sprinkled', 'willow herbs mixed with the roots of mountain flax', 'juice crushed from the nightshade berry'.

Such were the secrets found in the 'Book of Shadows' – a witch's bible – recorded there by those who learned to write. And when the witch lay dying it was taken from its hiding place and entrusted to a descendant gifted with the second sight, or burned so that the uninitiated could never tamper with forbidden knowledge.

One Knowing One is remembered as William Dawson, who inherited the mystic records of the Wise Man of Stokesley, long the oracle of South Durham and Cleveland, who flourished there at the beginning of the nineteenth century. Simple folk sought his counsel when they were troubled with mysteries beyond their understanding, or were tormented by fearful happenings. Many are the tales of his exploits.

There was once a farmer whose cattle were plagued with sickness. All day long the cows lay listless in the byre, with a plaintive lowing and saliva hanging from their mouths. His oxen, too, were out of sorts, kneeling before the plough, and no whip would stir them to their feet.

So it was to the Knowing One the farmer went, bearing gifts of cheese and new-laid eggs.

'Could it be some bogle is about his mischief?' the sage wondered. 'Perhaps a hag has put a curse upon the beasts. It will take but a few hours of darkness to fathom out the truth of it.'

59

Then, after consulting the pages of his leather-bound book, he spelled out the instructions for an experiment by which they could discover whether the cattle were truly bewitched.

At nightfall the farmer was to open wide the byre door, and inside to lay upon an iron platter a number of knots gouged from the bough of a rowan tree. They were to be arranged in a circle and left untouched until the first cock crowed. If then the rowan knots were found in disorder it was a sure sign of witchery.

LUCIFER, Empereur.

BELZÉBUT, Prince.

ASTAROT, Grand-duc.

LUCIFUGÉ, prem. Ministr.

SATANACHIA, grand général.

AGALIAREPT., aussi général.

FLEURETY, lieutenantgén.

SARGATANAS, brigadier.

NEBIROS, mar. de camp.

Authoritative portraits of Demons from a book published in Avignon in 1522.

When morning came the farmer went again to the Knowing One. 'At first light I returned to the byre and found the knots of wood squañered all about,' he explained. The worried farmer could not disguise his anxiety, and wondered what he should do to break the spell.

Once more the Knowing One searched through the pages of his bible, and there was prescribed an odd ritual – the antidote to be performed precisely as it was written.

It began in the still of night behind the closed door of the byre. A fire was lit of witchwood kindling, and in its flames was roasted the heart of a black hen pierced all over with pins. There was a spitting and sizzling as the blood dripped into the fire. Then an incantation spelled out in the Book of Shadows was recited, 'four times in a whisper, and three times more in a voice raised loud . . .'

When the heart of the fowl was shrivelled almost to a cinder, the farmer touched it with his poker and watched it crumble to ashes.

No sooner had this been done than he heard the clatter of hoofs and the rumble of wheels hurtling down the paved causey outside, as though a horse-drawn carriage were being driven furiously along. When the galloping ceased there came a pounding on the byre door, so violent that the timbers shook, and the farmer took refuge in the corner.

The pounding went on incessantly until the last spark of the fire went out. When only the smouldering ashes remained, whatever raged outside abandoned its attempt to enter. For a while there was silence, and then the sound of the carriage and horses could be heard fading away in the distance.

In the morning the cows were munching contentedly in their stalls. And when evening came, furrows long and straight ran across the fields.

✳   ✳   ✳

It was understandable that Anne became a timid child, always afraid to be left alone. Her widowed mother was an insensitive woman, determined that her daughter should be obedient and chaste, and taught the girl right from wrong more with fear than compassion.

Whenever Anne was mischievous she was threatened with Old

Harrow-Tooth, a mythical hag who lurked in dark corners, waiting to smother wayward children beneath the folds of her heavy cloak, or grind their bones with her sharp teeth.

'Listen!' her mother would whisper, with a finger to her lips. 'I hear Old Harrow-Tooth calling from under the stairs! "Fetch her to me," I hear her say. "Open the cupboard door and push her in!" '

Then Anne would be quiet, not daring to speak or shed another tear. Trembling, she would climb the stairs to bed, imagining that a withered hand would stretch out from the darkness and clutch at her nightdress.

She was never to tell lies, for then her tongue would stick fast to the roof of her mouth. She was never to wander far at play, nor smile at the gipsies on the moor. And never, *never* was she to pick wild flowers near the river banks, for there Peg the Prowler would be waiting. It was Peg who haunted the murky waters – a horrid goblin who lured unwary children close to the edge and dragged them down into her subaqueous den among the reeds.

'Peg the Prowler will get you if you wander there!' her mother would warn, describing a creature in long green tresses like a tangle of slimy weeds, and the foam floating on the surface near eddying pools as 'Peg Prowler's suds'.

It was no wonder that Anne lay awake in bed, imagining a bogle with beckoning finger and whirlpool eyes or a cloaked harridan stealing from the shadows of her room. Often she would wake from a nightmare, screaming, fighting for breath, as though she had just emerged from the depths of the river, or a heavy mantle had been suffocating her. Sometimes she would light the candle and keep watch through the hours of darkness, trembling whenever the floorboards creaked or a breath of wind outside the window seemed to whisper her name.

Anne's sleepless nights drew dark rings under her eyes. Her cheeks were pale, and she became so irritable that her mother feared the child was bewitched. 'Some Devil is up to its mischief!' she cried.

She tried a number of talismans to exorcize the spirit that possessed her daughter – red ribbon knotted to the bedpost, a branch of elder nailed above the cottage door, a twig of witch-wiggin made into a cross and stitched under the girl's dress. But nothing she tried drove the Devil away. Anne continued to be tormented by nightmares, and was fearful of every sound.

So it came about that one evening the widow and her daughter set off across the moor in search of the house of the Knowing One. It was dusk when they knocked at his door. He invited them into a darkened room which had a variety of charms hanging on the walls, and a pentagram crudely chalked on the floor. The curtains were closed, and only a glow from the fire lit the room.

He listened patiently to the woman's story, sometimes taking the girl's hands and gazing into her eyes. From what he heard and the symptoms he observed it was clear to him that the sufferer was under some mysterious spell.

When the child's history of nightmares and depression had been disclosed, he lit the lamp and set it on the table beside his Book of Shadows where he might find some formula to dispel the sorcery.

'He patiently listened to the woman's story,
sometimes taking the girl's hands and gazing closely into her eyes.'

For a long time the book lay open as he deciphered the secrets recorded in its pages, muttering the words over and over. Anne left her chair and stood close to her mother's side, each minute growing more apprehensive at the solemnity of the occasion and the mystery of it all.

At length the room was prepared for the ritual to be performed. The lamp was extinguished, and burning candles were placed around the pentagram drawn on the floor. Salt was sprinkled on the flames until the mystic confines flared green and blue, with thunderous shadows beyond.

As the Knowing One approached, Anne clung to her mother, muttering her protests. But with a smile of reassurance the sage unlocked her fingers and drew her towards the flames. One by one each article of her clothing was unfastened and thrown into a heap, until she stood there naked, trembling in his grasp.

He took the girl in his arms and carried her inside the fiery pentagram, where he annointed her forehead, eyelids, lips and breasts with a sweet-smelling ungent, all the while reciting some monotonous verse he had memorized from the book. Then he hugged her close to his body, his arms wrapped tightly around her, until her back arched and she was staring up into his face. Then he swung her around, moving in turn to each of the five points of his magic sign. 'Out, damned spirit!' his ceremony concluded. 'Out, I say!'

It was dark when they left the house across the moor, pausing for a moment at the doorway while the woman fumbled in her pocket for some coins to reward the Knowing One. And as they hurried on their way, Anne was relieved to peep back over her shoulder and see the lamplight in his window grow faint.

It is likely that if, by chance, some demon had come to possess her, then now it had surely been driven away. As for Anne's fearful dreams, these recurred throughout her childhood. Many a night she woke with a fright when Old Harrow-Tooth or Peg the Prowler had come in her nightmares to seek her out. But more often it was the memory of a fiery pentagram and the lasting offence to her modesty that kept her from sleep.

North Country Brags

In ancient British history a Brag is described as a Pan, Silenus or
Satyr. But its Celtic definition is an untruth or *breugach* – a
deceitful female who can assume various shapes and disguises.

Long ago, in the county of Durham, it was often tales of the
breugach or brag that spread fear among the villagers.

'Lister's Out!'

In the village of Hedworth there once lived an old woman called
Lister. No one knew her given name, for she had no friends or
relatives that the old folk could remember. If anyone had dared
knock upon the door of her shack, a forbidding crone with sharp
eyes would have peeped out at them.

None of the villagers would pass the time of day with her; and
some picked their way around the edge of the swamp rather than
venture near her dwelling place. She went out only after nightfall,
disguising herself in a variety of forms so that no one would ever
discover the perpetrator of the mischief she caused.

Early one morning a farmer was awakened by the lowing of
cattle and the squawking of hens. When he went to investigate the
disturbance his torchlight showed the cows drained and sickly, and
chicken feathers scattered all about. He saw no poacher prowling
there, no fox slinking from the coop.

Then, perched in the eaves of the byre, his light shone on some
winged predator of uncommon proportions, alert as an eagle on a
cliff-top. The gleam of his torch was reflected in its eyes as it stared
at him before flying off through the open door.

Elsewhere in the county a scarecrow was seen moving about the
fields, waving its arms, spitting and crying out like a monstrous

cat. Dale mists were sometimes seen swirling to human form, appearing in a shroud of grey as it drifted over the ground.

When such mysterious sights were reported, the villagers explanation was always the same. 'It's Aud Lister prowling about!' they would say, for few were spared her mischief, and never those who roused her anger.

Then came the night when three villains were returning home after long hours of drinking at the tavern. They were attracted by a glow in the window of the old woman's shack. Peering in, they saw only the logs smouldering in the grate and a sack of straw on which she slept.

'Lister's out and about her devilry!' said one. And they looked around in the moonlight for some sign of her on the moor.

It was at the edge of the swamp nearby where they caught sight of a dark shape leaping among the reeds. The mugs of ale and several drams of whisky made them bold. They ran off in pursuit, crying like banshees as they bounded through the heather, 'Witch! Snaggle-toothed whore! Found you at last!'

For a while the reeds were still and the frogs ceased croaking. Then they saw it again – a wraith-like figure coming toward them.

Seventeenth-century woodcuts of witches.

'Lister!' they breathed, lying in wait as she approached. When their quarry was near they emerged from their hiding place and sprang upon the spectre, thrusting it down into the swamp. There was a cry of alarm and a fearful struggle ensued as the assailants strove to hold their captive beneath the surface. During the fray the blackened features of an old woman emerged momentarily, and her hands were seen clutching at the reeds. But again and again her cries were stifled in the slimy marsh.

At last the struggling was over for a while. Then the old woman, or whatever they held in their grasp, began to writhe and convulse with a ferocity that startled them. Their arms were bitten and clawed as though some feral cat were fighting to break loose. They were forced to release their hold, and a feline form reared above the surface, its eyes glowing, its teeth bared. Growling and spitting it tore at its tormentors with a fury that struck terror into their hearts. And it was not until they lay sprawled in the swamp nursing their wounds that it drifted off across the moor in the direction of the old woman's shack.

That night Aud Lister's curse had fallen upon the three villains. But the doctor and the wise men of the village thought it more likely that they had been cornered by a rabid beast. In the days that followed, each of the victims was stricken with fits of madness during which they were plagued with hallucinations. And although they burned with fever, and a fire raged in their throats, they were afraid to moisten their lips, for their most fearful dread was the sound and touch of water.

Old Bogglebo

In the north country witches were sometimes called boggleboes. This was the name given to a woman from Hylton. It was thought that she had no home of her own, because she was always seen roaming the streets of the village or begging at the market place in Sunderland. There was nothing much about her clothes, and at that time any penurious woman who lived out-of-doors and wandered from place to place was thought to be a witch. So, to the villagers of Hylton and the stall keepers at the market, she was known as Old Bogglebo.

Jock the keelman remembered that it was a stormy day when the woman came along asking that he take her across the water to Sunderland. The wind hurled silvery spray upon the quay, and the keels all lay fast moored.

'Don't fret about the black sky and angry swell,' she told him. 'No harm will come to you.' Voices in the wind always whispered to her and warned her of impending danger, she promised.

The keelman shook his head, and she saw his lips set grim. In such a storm his craft would surely be torn to shreds.

The woman's eyes held him in her stare. 'Listen to the voices of the squall. They tell of a safe journey and good fortune for the boatman who helps a traveller on her way.'

Jock heard the wind howl, and his lips pursed tighter still.

Old Bogglebo looked up into the sky, listening again to the wailing and moaning. 'You hear what the voices call? Safe journey for a kindness, and a watery grave for he who turns a voyager away!'

She told how the voices foretold his doom should he refuse to venture to sea: how some day Old Neptune would dash his boat upon the rocks and reach up to drag him down into the depths. A curse on him should he not relent.

Jock was as superstitious as he was stubborn. Perhaps it was fear of the bogle's vengeance or a lull in the storm that persuaded him to untie his keel and take to the water.

'There's no danger,' the woman urged. 'Run along full sail. Don't take the reef. The wind will guide us true.'

Then she hunched into the huddock at the stern and lay there snug, chuckling at the sailor's fears.

Once unleashed, the boat sped along swift and straight as an arrow. The sails fluttered and cracked, billowing forward whichever way the helm was turned. The bows cut through the swell with unusual thrust, and a silvery wake trailed true as a falling star. The wind moaned and shrilled, rousing the sea to rage. Black clouds raced overhead while Old Bogglebo's shoulders rocked with laughter.

Fast and faster still the keel hastened on its voyage, one moment lunging through the angry sea, the next flying above the breakers. And above it all a voice from the stern could be heard shrieking with excitement.

A wizard on a cat's back.

When, at last, their destination appeared over the bows, the woman was nowhere to be found. Instead, the startled keelman caught sight of a black cat leaping from the huddock and clinging to the mast.

Humbleknowe Brag

It was in the evening one winter when a beggar woman knocked on the door of a country house near Sedgefield, beyond the River Tees. At her side stood a little girl, huddled close to hide from the biting wind. As the door opened the light from the hall fell upon them, and a maidservant appeared on the threshold.

'If you would be so kind – a place to shelter for the night?' the visitor muttered. 'A bundle of straw to lie on in the stable. It's so cold out on the moor.'

The servant hurried back inside, and presently her master came to the doorway clutching the collar of his dog.

'Be on your way!' he said bitterly. 'There's no shelter here for strangers!'

'Then spare a crust of bread for the bairn,' the woman pleaded.

But the man was unrelenting. His dog growled and bared its teeth.

The beggar stared hard and long at the master of the house, and wistfully into the warm glow beyond the hall. Her parting warning was almost lost in the sighing of the winter wind. 'Remember two homeless souls when you're snug around the hearth. Make fast the windows and bolt the doors, because the nights are dark and long!'

As the winter wore on, the visitors who came knocking and begging for food and shelter were forgotten. Then, one night, when the lady of the house was sitting beside the fire waiting for her husband to return from his business in town, she heard the sound of a horses hoofs clip-clopping across the yard towards the stable.

'Sarah, unfasten the bolt. Your master is home at last,' she called.

The dog moved from the hearth, but did not wag its tail nor hurry to the door. Instead it crept under the table and lay there whimpering.

Minutes passed, and no further sound was heard. From the doorway the servant looked out into the moonlit yard. But there was no sign of horse or rider, and the stable door was closed. After a time of waiting and watching she closed the door again, assuming her mistress had been mistaken.

It was almost midnight when the clatter of hoofs was heard once more. Along the gravel path they came and upon the cobblestones at the back of the house, louder now, as though several horses were approaching. Round and round the house they galloped in headlong flight.

Sarah and her mistress peeped through the window, but they saw nothing outside in the moonlight, although the sound of the thundering hoofs continued. Then came a pounding on the door, and a howling in the chimney set the fire blazing.

Stricken with fear, they listened to the mysterious sounds grow louder. Smoke billowed from the grate, and the lamp went dim. It seemed a long time before the haunting ceased and the house was quiet again.

The master did not return that night, but was brought home the following morning by some farm workers who found him at the roadside. He remembered that his horse was startled by the approach of a wild herd galloping over the moor. His mount reared, throwing him to the ground where for two hours or more he lay unconscious. And had his feeble cries not been heard he would surely have perished in the biting winter wind.

The Witches of Pendle Forest

A cart trundled along the Trough of Bowland, winding its way through the wooded hills. Bound inside were three generations of witches. This was their last journey. They were travelling to a dungeon in Lancaster Castle – to imprisonment and the gallows.

Two days later, on a summer morning in the year 1612, they were herded through the crowded streets, oblivious of the jeering townsfolk and the voice of a parson who walked before them.

'May God have mercy on their souls,' he cried. 'His love is everlasting and His mercy knows no bounds.' It was a plea of bitter irony, for they had been shown no mercy in this world.

The story of the witches of Pendle Forest begins about two years earlier when Mother Demdike, a blind old woman, was resting on the arm of her granddaughter, Alizon. She was leading her away from the house of a miller who clenched his fist and called after them. 'Away from here, worthless witches. I've not even a mouldy crust of bread for servants of the Devil!'

The woman stumbled on the path, and the young girl trembled at his fury. The miller pursued them to the gate, waving his arms angrily. 'A length of rope is what I'd gladly give, to knot around your necks!'

Mother Demdike's eyes could not reflect the hate smouldering within her. 'I'd wish you in your grave,' she called back, 'but your heart is dead already. Watch to your daughter. Watch out for the one you hold dear. Old Tibbs will be coming to seek her out!'

Before the season changed, the miller's daughter became pale and sickly. She was never to live to the see the bluebells bloom again in spring. And one curious feature neighbours remembered – whenever she was alone a stray black cat had come to keep her company. It had followed her around the garden and along the banks of the mill stream, brushing its face and neck against her ankles, its tail high and bushy.

Mother Demdike made no secret of the vengeance she sought. She chuckled to herself whenever she and Alizon passed the miller's door, squeezing her granddaughter's hand and asking, 'Do you see her, my love? Is she alone in the garden? Tibbs will find her for sure.'

It was an incident that happened the following summer which led to the arrest and trial of the Pendle witches. On this occasion Alizon asked a pedlar for some pins and ribbon to make her hair look pretty. But he did not understand the dreams of a young girl. Even sparkling jewels, he taunted, could never change a devil to an angel.

Her grandmother had taught her well the art of witchery. Alizon put a curse on the pedlar that Satan would take him. And before he had passed out of sight it seemed that the Evil One struck. He reeled and fell to the ground, scattering his charms and trinkets all about him. According to one account 'his head was drawn awrie, his eyes and face deformed, his speech not well to bee understood, and his legs starcke lame . . .' Unfortunately for the girl, he survived his affliction long enough to point out the mischief-maker to the local magistrate.

Boastfully, and with vivid detail, Alizon described how she had put a curse on the pedlar, for she was too young and naive to realize the consequence of her confession. Before her deposition was over she had implicated her neighbours and family. It was her grandmother, she told them, who had taught them all the wiles of witchcraft.

Among the old woman's willing disciples was Alizon's mother, described as a wild, squint-eyed woman. Damned, too, were her half-wit brother, James, and another grandchild, nine-year-old Jennet.

Prominent among the neighbours indicted for witchery was Old Chattox, a withered widow, toothless and bent with age. It so happened that for a long time a feud had existed between the Chattox and Demdike families. And now, as they accused one another of past mischief, a chronicle of their misdeeds was brought to light.

It was learned how they desecrated graves, met in covens to commune with imps and devils, and once contrived to destroy Lancaster Castle by means of witchcraft. It was revealed that

Mother Demdike's familiar spirit, a black cat called Tibbs, had tormented the miller's daughter, and Old Chattox had bewitched a family near Colne, bringing sickness and death to the wife and children. In condemning each other they were drawing the hangman's noose tighter around their own throats. Few of their wicked deeds were left uncovered.

And so it was that the witches of Pendle Forest were carted away along the Trough of Bowland. They were not afraid, because they did not then realize how cruelly they were to suffer under the new laws of James I.

Only one was to cheat the hangman. Succumbing to age and infirmity, Mother Demdike died in Lancaster Castle gaol.

Altogether, ten simple-minded peasant folk, including three generations of one family, paid the ultimate penalty that August day. There were many who believed that their only crime was to be poor and ignorant – easy prey for the relentless persecutors of the seventeenth century.

The execution of witches in England in the 17th century.
The witch finder is seen receiving his wages for discovering them.

The Goodwife of Laggan

In the Scottish highlands there once lived a fearless hunter. Legend tells that he drove the Devil from Kingussie and banished Lamh Dhearg, the ghost of Glenmore Forest. From Loch Maree to Loch Earn no witch or demon could prevail against the Hunter of Badenoch, for he and his faithful dogs were devoted to ridding the Highlands of Satan and his disciples.

One evening, while roaming the hills on his crusade, a storm swept in from the sea, and he was forced to take shelter in a herdsman's hut. When darkness descended he lit a fire and settled there for the night.

He was awakened from his sleep when the dogs growled at a scratching on the door. He quietened them and listened. Then it came again – a clawing and a scratching, followed by a plaintive cry, clearly audible above the howling wind and the rain lashing against the roof.

When he opened the door there was nothing to be seen. A black cat, unseen in the darkness, slid past him and moved towards the warmth of the fire.

The dogs' ears pricked again, and they sprang forward, sniffing around in confusion because the interloper could not be found. After a time the hunter shrugged his shoulders and returned to his bundle of straw, and the dogs settled down at his feet.

While they all slept, the cat emerged from the shadows and sat before the fire, licking a paw to groom its fur. Had he awakened again, the Hunter of Badenoch would have been astonished to watch the creature transform, each moment growing taller, standing on its hind legs and arching its back, its fur trailing to the floor. Whiskers and tail vanished as its proportions increased, until now it was the silhouette of a woman who stood there, wearing a poke bonnet and flowing gown.

It was the dogs that sensed her presence. Snarling and baring their teeth they held the intruder at bay against the wall beside the fire.

Their master stared in disbelief to see a woman kicking at the dogs, her arms raised before her face. 'Pity, sir!' he heard her cry. 'Call them off! I mean you no harm.'

He grasped the animals by their scruffs, one in each hand, while the woman shuffled into the firelight. When the flames lit up her face he gasped with surprise, recognizing her as the Goodwife of Laggan, a meek old woman, known for her virtue and her kindness to neighbours who lived in a nearby village.

'Hold them fast!' she cried again. 'I came in only to shelter from the storm. Tie your dogs to the beam where they cannot break free.' From under her gown she drew a rope with which he could bind them. It was long and coarse, like plaited strands of hair. 'Fasten them tight!' she urged. 'They are wild with the scent of my blood!'

The hunter wound the rope around the dogs' necks and hitched it to the beam. But, suspicious of her wandering after dark and the woman's mysterious appearance there, he tied the knot loosely.

When this was done and the beasts were held at bay, fear was gone from the eyes of the Goodwife of Laggan. Instead they burned with hate and her manner became menacing.

'I seek you out in the Devil's name!' she threatened, hissing like a snake poised to strike. 'This morning in the loch I drowned one who has long persecuted the servants of our master, the Prince of Darkness. Now your hour has come!'

With her fingers crooked like talons, she flew at the hunter's throat. With a cry he fell back, fighting to fend off her ferocious attack.

In their master's defence the dogs leapt towards the witch, breaking the knot which fastened them. In a fury they tore at her gown until blood streamed from her arm.

'Hold fast! Hold fast!' she shrieked. And the plaited strands of hair twisted so tightly around the beam that the timber smouldered. But the dogs were free to snarl and snap, despite her kicking and clawing.

The witch's struggle to fight them off was in vain. Torn and bleeding, she cursed the beasts and retreated toward the fire. There her tattered gown fell in a heap, and from beneath its folds a raven took flight, squawking and fluttering into the breast of the chimney.

When the storm was over, the hunter made his way in haste to the village. There he found the Goodwife of Laggan lying in her bed, with anxious neighbours gathered around. That evening she had been seen wandering the hills in search of peat. But it was long after nightfall when she returned, wild-eyed and breathless.

'A witch is here among us!' the hunter declared, pulling back the blanket to reveal her bleeding limbs. He told the startled neighbours of his encounter in a herdsman's shack; of her confessed homage to the Prince of Darkness.

At the doorway the dogs' hackles rose, for now it was not the Goodwife of Laggan who stared at them from her bed. The witch's eyes burned like candle flames, her lips twisting in a devilish grimace. Screeching with laughter she cursed all those gathered around her bed and called out an entreaty to the Evil One.

Possessed with fear and anger, the neighbours bound the hag to her bed, stifled her screams with a pillow, and burnt her where she lay.

Later that night two travellers on their way from Badenoch were astonished to come upon a wraith-like figure fleeing along the road towards the churchyard, her clothes engulfed in flames. They swore that the ghost was pursued by a masked rider on a black horse whose nostrils flared and hoofs thundered through the glen. As the fiery figure was overtaken, the rider bent low to seize his captive and lay her across the saddle. Then, with a triumphant cry, he galloped off into the hills.

For the past three hundred years the haunting has remained a mystery. For a long time it was believed that the ghost of the Goodwife of Laggan was seeking refuge and sanctuary in Dalarossie churchyard, while the Evil One, mounted on his black steed, was determined to claim her as his own.

A Curse on the King

One All Hallows Eve towards the end of the sixteenth century, a sinister congregation assembled at a church in North Berwick on the southern coast of the Firth of Forth. Their ceremony was not in praise of God, but to pay homage to their master, the Devil. Those in attendance were a coven of witches, gathered together on their festive eve.

They had travelled from the corners of East Lothian and beyond, some making their way across the water, with flagons of wine to rouse their spirits on the journey.

The North Berwick coven, 1591: members drink in a cellar,
another takes down the words of the Devil preaching from a pulpit,
others boil up a cauldron to create a storm and sink a ship at sea.

In the churchyard they danced among the tombstones to the haunting notes of a Jew's harp. 'Cummer, go ye before,' they chanted. 'Cummer, go ye. If ye will not go before, cummer, let me.'

Later, when the church doors were shut and black candles burned, it was the Devil who stood in the pulpit. He looked a fearful sight, wrapped in a black gown, with talons clasped about his chest, smouldering eyes, and horns protruding from his head.

All vowed allegiance to him, and swore to obey his commands. At this meeting each was enlisted to a special mission – to rid Satan of his mortal enemy, King James VI of Scotland.

At the master's side was Francis, Earl of Bothwell, a cousin to the king, and heir-apparent to the throne. He was the leader of the coven and had good cause to see the Evil One's task done. Beside the Earl stood Dr Fian, a schoolmaster of the county. As clerk to all in the master's service, he was appointed to keep a register of those in attendance, and to mark well the faint-hearted who stayed away. It was he that had ridden to the church with the Devil's candles flaring from the head of his horse.

During that autumn and winter, witches of the coven gathered in groups at secret rendezvous to perform the Devil's work.

At Prestonpans they met in a secluded glen by moonlight. There they moulded a wax image with a laurel fixed to its head. From hand to hand the witch-doll was passed, fingers clutching at its throat and curses breathed upon it. Briars pierced its heart before this likeness of the king lost its shape as it was held close to the fire.

At Leith a huddle of witches stared out to sea. They grasped the scruff of a stray cat, captured in an alley. The frightened creature spat and scratched because on its paws were fastened gobbets of flesh torn from the body of a man found hanging from a gibbet. Curses were muttered, and then, with a cry of terror, the cat was flung from the bank into the waters of the Firth of Forth – a macabre ceremony to raise a storm.

Presently the skies darkened and a wind stirred the sea to a fury. The witches chuckled as they watched a boat sailing towards the shore founder in a sudden squall. They didn't know then that it was not the vessel on which James was returning home with his bride from Denmark.

The plot to bring about the death of the king would have

remained a secret had it not been betrayed by a maidservant, remembered as Gilly Duncan.

Suspicious of her strange behaviour and her prowling at night, her master questioned the girl thoroughly. But it was not until he had threatened to punish her and dismiss her from his service that she confessed to communing with the Devil and attending the grand sabbats of East Lothian's witches.

Many conspirators were implicated as the story unfolded, but few were brought to trial for sorcery and treason.

For many hours Dr John Fian was subjected to torture in the county gaol. His fingers were broken in the thumbscrews; his legs crushed in the iron boot. Needles were thrust under his nails until he writhed in agony. Groans and screams escaped his lips, but never a word of confession. Although racked with torture, perhaps he feared more the vengeance of Satan. It is recorded that finally he was strangled and his body burned on Castle Hill in Edinburgh.

Agnes Sampson, a midwife of Keith, together with Euphemia MacLean, a woman of noble birth, was questioned by James himself. They told how they had attempted to bribe a servant from the royal household to steal a garment worn by the king. This they

King James I, when King James VI of Scotland,
examining the accused in the North Berwick witch trials of the 1590s.

would have smeared with the venom of a toad, so that when it was worn again it would, by black magic, summon the angel of death.

Both women were damned when Agnes whispered words that had passed between the king and his bride when they were alone on their wedding night. Who, but a witch, James reasoned, could unveil such a secret. That winter they were also put to death on Castle Hill.

History recalls that neither charm nor curse brought about the downfall of the king who later became James I of England. As for Francis Hepburn, Earl of Bothwell and prime instigator of the plot, it is said that he fled to Italy where he died in poverty many years later.

The Witches' Reel

This is the song that the North Berwick witches sang as they danced. ('Cummer' was a Scottish word used for addressing a woman, particularly a witch.)

> Cummer, go ye before, cummer, go ye.
> If ye willna go before, cummer, let me.
>   Ring-a-ring a-widdershins
>   Linkin' lithely widdershins
> Cummer carlin crone and queen
>   Roun' go we!
>
> Cummer, go ye before, cummer, go ye.
> If ye willna go before, cummer, let me.
>   Ring-a-ring a-widdershins
>   loupin' lightly widdershins
> Kilted coats and fleeing hair
>   Three times three.
>
> Cummer, go ye before, cummer, go ye.
> If ye willna go before, cummer, let me.
>   Ring-a-ring a-widdershins
>   Whirlin' Skirlin' widdershins
> And de'il take the hindmost
>   Who'er she be!

Maiden of Auldearn

In the wake of dour Calvinism which swept the north-east of Scotland in the sixteenth century, when it was believed that 'Auld Hornie', the Devil, dug pitfalls for unwary sinners, there lived at Auldearn a young woman named Isobel Gowdie. Describing herself as the Maiden, a disciple of Satan, she was either truly a witch or a girl gifted with the most vivid imagination.

'Black John' and the witches from the *Confession of Isobel Gowde* as depicted in George Cruikshank's illustration to Scott's *Letters on Demonology and Witchcraft*, 1830.

At her trial before the Sheriff of Auldearn, apparently without threats of torture, she freely confessed to consorting with the 'meikle black man'; to her participation in satanic orgies on the desolate hills beyond Auldearn; and to the weaving of infernal spells.

Her story began one night when she was wandering alone between the Heads and the farmsteads of Drumdewin.

'There I met the Devil and made a covenant with him. And I promised to meet him in the night at the kirk of Auldearn . . . And there I denied my baptism, putting one hand on my crown and the other on the sole of my foot, giving all between my two hands to the Devil.

'He stood at the reader's desk with a black book in his hand. Margaret Brodie held me up to the Devil to be baptized by him. And he marked me on the shoulder, sucking out my blood and spitting into his hand. Sprinkling the blood on my head he said, "I baptize thee Janet in my own name."

'After a time we went away. The next time I met him was in the New Ward of Inshoch. And there we were lovers . . . He was a black, hairy man. His embraces were rough and his lips as cold as spring water. Sometimes he wore boots, but when his feet were bare I could see they were forked and cloven . . .'

At her trial in April 1662, the Maiden of Auldearn further confessed that she and other witches of her coven had learned to fly through the air on magic straws.

'I had a little horse, and would say, "Horse and hattock in the devil's name." And then we would fly away wherever we wanted to go, just as straws fly in the wind. Wild straws and cornstalks serve as horses for us. And we put them between our legs, saying, "Horse and hattock in the Devil's name."

'We will see dead at our pleasure anyone who spies us flying on straws and forgets to bless himself. Their souls will go to Heaven, but their bodies remain and fly as horses for us, as small as straws.'

She related how they held their meetings about the end of each quarter, thirteen in number, counting the Master. At these sabbats each member had a spirit who was summoned at will, to wait upon them and do their bidding. Isobel could distinguish one from another, though they were all of like appearance, spindle-limbed with heads disproportionate. Their eyes shone bright as berries, and each wore an impish grin.

The women of the coven were known by special names, given them by the Master. There was Bessie Wilson of Auldearn, nicknamed 'Throw-the-corn-yard'. She was favoured with two spirits to wait upon her – 'Rorie' and 'Thief-of-Hell-Wait-upon-

Herself', both clad in yellow. 'Robert the Jack', an awkward, half-witted fool, was chosen to tend to the whims of Bessie Hay, familiarly called 'Able and Stout'.

Jean Martin, appointed the coven's Register (secretary) was known as 'Over-the-Dyke-with-it', because whenever they danced at orgies the Master would take her hand, and as they leapt and reeled he would cry out time and again, 'Over the dyke with it . . .' Her little devil was 'MacHector', always clad in grass-green.

Then there was Margaret Wilson – 'Pickle-nearest-the-Wind', Elsbet Nishie – 'Bessie Bauld', and their attendant spirits, 'Swein' and 'Roaring Lion'. Answering Isobel's call was the spirit 'Reed River', who dressed all in black.

'Many were the devils waiting upon us,' Isobel explained, 'but none more awful than the Master Devil, and we all pay reverence to him.'

She told of their spells used for metamorphosis. 'Into cats and hares and jackdaws we can change, to steal through the night or run like the wind or skirt the treetops. When we want to change into a crow we say three times:

> I shall go into a crow,
> With sorrow and such, and a black thraw!
> And I shall go in the Devil's name
> Until I come home again.'

To all manner of maleficium Isobel Gowdie freely confessed, as though she had been favoured with rare knowledge which she was eager to share with others.

'Before Candlemas we went to the east of Kinloss, and there we yoked a plough drawn by frogs . . . John Young of Mebestown drove the plough, and the frogs pulled like oxen. Traces by which they were harnessed were made of dog grass. The blade in front of the plough-share was made from the horn of a ram. Twice round in a circle we went, praying to the Devil that the fruit of the land be blighted, and that briars and thistles might grow there . . .'

Of the curse they put upon the children of a Laird who had set his dogs on them, she disclosed:

'John Taylor brought home the clay in the fold of his plaid. His wife poured water on it in the Devil's name, and made it soft like hasty-pudding. Then she moulded images of the Laird's sons with it. Each doll had all the parts and marks of a child – head, eyes, nose, hands, feet, and mouth with little lips; and the hands were folded down to its sides. It was as big as a flayed sucking-pig.

'We laid the doll's face to the fire until it shrivelled with the heat; and we put clear flames around it until it burned red as fire . . . We roasted it now and then. Every other day there would be a part of it well baked. It was never found and crumbled, so the Laird's sons were made to suffer by it . . .'

Although it was claimed that their witchcraft brought about the suffering and death of the Laird of Park's sons, something went awry with the spell they cast on the children of the Laird of Lochley.

In effecting this curse they boiled together gobbets of flesh from dogs and sheep. For long hours the brew was stirred, and then strewn along the paths where the children would tread. Perhaps their spell lacked potency, or maybe the children did not pass that way. Whatever the reason, their intended victims remained unharmed.

'There were spells to recite while moulding the images and casting them into the fire,' Isobel continued. 'Over each one we would chant together . . . The Devil taught us the words, and when we had learned them we all fell down upon our bare knees, with our hair over our eyes and our arms raised, gazing upon the Devil. Thrice the words are said, even while the dolls singe and spit . . .'

Sometimes the Auldearn coven held dominion over the wind on land and sea. 'When we raise the wind,' she said, 'we take a piece of cloth and wet it in water. And we take a washerwoman's beetle and beat the cloth on a stone, saying three times:

> I beat this cloth upon this stone
> To raise the wind in the Devil's name.
> It shall not be allayed until I please again.

'When we lay the wind we dry the rag and say three times:

> We lay the wind in the Devil's name.
> It shall not rise until we wish to raise it again.

'And if the wind will not lie instantly, we call upon our spirits and say to them, "Thief! Thief! Conjure the wind and cause it to lie!"

'We have no power over rain, but can raise the wind whenever we please . . .

'Our Master has power beyond your dreams!' declared the Maiden of Auldearn. 'He made us believe that there is no God but him . . .'

The fate of Isobel Gowdie is not recorded. But it is likely that she was remembered each Hallowe'en at nearby Balmoral. There, until the middle of the last century, it was customary to light a bonfire beside the castle walls on the last evening of October. An effigy of a witch was burnt as a symbol of triumph over the powers of darkness.

Heralded by pipers, this life-size image – the 'Shandy Dann' – was wheeled on a cart, as were the witches of old, to its funeral pyre. There was silence for a time, while the indictment was read to the gathered clansmen. Then, amid wild cheering and the skirl of pipes, the 'Shandy Dann' was condemned and plunged into the fires of Hell.

The Bridle

There were once two brothers who worked as blacksmiths at a village in the Border region of Scotland. They were handsome lads, with bright blue eyes and fiery hair, and they were as happy as the day is long.

So hard did they toil from morning till dusk – and with many a dram after supper – that they slept soundly at night, never waking until the sun showed in the sky.

Then there came a time when the younger brother lost the sparkle in his eyes. Day by day he grew more weary, with hardly the strength to wield the hammer. And the older brother was distressed to see him wasting away.

'It's a lassie who comes to me in my dreams and keeps me from my sleep,' the younger brother explained one day. He told of a girl with raven locks and eyes that held him spellbound. Quiet as the moonlight she would steal into his room whenever he closed his eyes. There she would whisper his name, kiss him gently and entice him to follow her out into the night.

For a long time he would tell no more, because he had promised the girl of his dreams that no one should hear of his adventures after dark. And so his eyes grew hollow, his cheeks pale, and often he would toss and turn in his bed, crying out in his sleep.

As the days wore on, he became more and more listless. He lost his appetite, and some mornings he was too tired to climb from his bed. At last he could hide the secret no longer.

It was then that his older brother learned that the beguiling lassie who came at night was in truth a witch. Her gentle touch and soft brown eyes hid a heart of stone. Each night, when she had lured the young one from his room, she took him to the stable and there slipped a bridle over his head. By some mysterious spell she was able at once to transform him into a lively stallion with a chestnut mane on whose back she might travel fast wheresoever she wished.

Over the hills and glens her mount would gallop. And, screeching with excitement, she would spur him on, with never a moment's rest. To a far-off place they would journey, where a coven met with their master, the Devil. There, panting and glistening with sweat, the beast was tethered to a tree until their revelry was over. And before the first cock crowed she would ride back again, unbridle the exhausted stallion, and, with the spell now wearing off, would leave in the stable a fatigued and bewildered young man.

Hearing of the young one's plight, the older brother was furious, and swore by all that was holy to break the spell.

The next time the witch came calling it was he who lay in his brother's place, peeping above the blanket. Silent as a wraith she entered the room through the window and stood beside the bed. He felt the touch of her hand and lips as she whispered to wake him from sleep. Her black hair fell over her eyes. Longer than usual she lingered there, for her kisses were exciting, and he was more resourceful an opportunist than his brother.

Eventually he followed out into the night along the path leading to the stable where she fastened the enchanted bridle to his head and shoulders. Almost at once the spell was cast. As had happened before, it was not the hand of a young man she held, but the reins of an excited stallion, its hoofs tearing at the ground, its chestnut mane shining in the moonlight.

With a shriek of delight the witch leapt on its back and spurred the beast to a gallop. Horse and rider sped off over the braes to the Devil's rendezvous. And in that sheltered glen far away the coven met to dance and weave their mischief.

While the witch was at her merry-making the stallion tugged and bit at its tether. Again and again it rubbed its head against the tree until the bridle fell away. Free at last, the beast melted into the darkness, and in its place the older brother stood, breathless and bewildered.

For a long time he hid in the shadows, waiting for his tormentor to return. When she appeared he crept up behind her and fastened the bridle about her head.

Her struggles were in vain, for instantly the spell fell upon her instead, changing her to a black mare, and her shrieking to a whinny. The avenger climbed on her back, digging his heels into her flanks so savagely that she set off at a furious gallop. Lashing out with the reins, he rode the mare along the roughest paths. Mile after mile he spurred her on, through hedges and over ditches, up the steepest slopes and headlong down the other side.

It was dawn when they reached the village, and the mare could barely drag one leg behind another. Its nostrils flared, its coat steamed, and froth bubbled from its mouth.

Some say that the blacksmith was merciless, and nailed iron shoes to the mare's bleeding hoofs. Others say that he took pity on the wretched beast, confident that the witch had learned her lesson. So he led the mare to the stable behind the forge. There he fed and watered her, bathed her wounds and let her rest a while. Then, well groomed and newly shod, she was set free to wander the banks and braes.

No one will ever know whether, at the end of its journey, the mare was shown compassion or cruelly driven away. But it is remembered that before the day had passed a dark-haired bonny lassie from over the hill was found in her bed, hugging the sheets about her, fearful that someone should find her there.

When neighbours ignored her shrieking protests and tore the sheets from her grasp, her body was seen to be bruised and scratched, and to each of her hands and feet a horseshoe was fastened.

Aberdeen Witches

Hundreds of years ago the wild moors and lonely hills and glens of Scotland were shrouded in mystery. It is a corner of the western world where stories of sorcery and witchery abound; and nowhere in Europe was the persecution of heresy more fervently pursued, nowhere did the fires blaze more fiercely.

During the sixteenth and seventeenth centuries, the courts of Scotland ignored the basic principle of Anglo-Saxon law which assumed that those accused were innocent until proved guilty. Where witchcraft was concerned, confessions were extracted by torture, and punishment was swift and merciless. The condemned were usually tied at a stake and burned alive. Some were strangled before their bodies were consigned to the flames.

Like most of the many Aberdeen witches, Janet Wishart was an aged crone. She was indicted for putting a curse on Alexander Thomson and Andrew Webster. Her victims were stricken with fits of shivering and high temperatures followed by lethargy and sweating – like fevers prevalent at that time. When the spell brought about the death of Webster, the fate of his tormentor was sealed.

The indictment referred to other acts of witchcraft committed by the old woman: curses which resulted in sickness or accident. A godless, ignorant wretch, heedless of the consequences of her testimony, she told of a variety of deeds involving spells and incantations. Most were very likely imagined, but they earned for her the reputation of being one of Scotland's most versatile witches.

Her examiners were led to believe that she used the dismembered bodies of felons found hanging from the gibbet for obscene and wicked purposes; invoked spirits from the graves of those not long interred; conjured snakes and monstrous cats to torment her

A procession of naked witches carrying a cat on a litter.

victims; and raised storms to blight crops by throwing burning coals into the air. There was no wickedness beyond the bounds of her master, the Prince of Darkness, she swore.

One of the Aberdeen witches who stood trial with Janet Wishart sought the leniency of the court by implicating others of her acquaintance. She denounced many of her neighbours, pointing them out and describing to the investigators where on their bodies the Devil's mark could be found. She exposed many others as the women she had seen at a witches' celebration at a glen in Atholl, where more than two hundred had been present. But the treacherous woman succeeded only in delaying her own execution and causing suffering to many innocent villagers.

An interesting feature of the Aberdeen trial records details the cost involved in executing those convicted. The account relates to the execution of Janet Wishart and Isobel Crocker, a woman who accompanied her to the pyre:

20 loads of peat to burn them	40 shillings
A boll (6 bushels) of coal	24 shillings
4 tar barrels	26 shillings & 8 pence
Fir and iron barrels	16 shillings & 8 pence
A stake and dressing of it	16 shillings
4 fathoms of tows (hangman's rope)	4 shillings
Carrying peat, coals and barrels to the hill	8 shillings & 4 pence
One Justice for their execution	13 shillings & 4 pence

At 75 shillings for the killing of each witch, it is understandable why poor communities found this an imposing tax on parish chests. It throws light on many of the practices prevalent three hundred years ago, when a shilling or two was a living wage. The law stipulated that the witch must contribute to the cost of her own execution, and that the rich were to bear the charges of punishing anyone who served them. It explains why wealthy men and women often fell victim to the witch-hunters.

Even when the kirk and local councils of the parish were required to find the means of execution, the financial burden did not dampen the resolution of ministers and elders to rid the community of anyone suspected of witchery.

The trial of the Aberdeen witches kindled a fire which blazed for many years. It spread throughout Scotland, embracing countless women whose only offence was to brew natural remedies for sickness or tell horoscopes by contemplating the position of heavenly bodies.

The Spells of Isobel Grierson

The casting of spells upon man and beast, by brewing potions or reciting simple incantations; the fashioning and melting of wax images to cause pain and suffering; invoking devils to wake children from their sleep – these were the alleged practices of the witches of England, which changed little over the centuries.

Records portray the witches of Scotland as weaving more imaginative spells to bring fresh torments to their victims. Such was the case of Isobel Grierson, wife of a labourer from Preston-pans, a burgh of East Lothian on the Firth of Forth, who was tried by the Criminal Tribunal of Edinburgh in 1607.

She was described as a vindictive woman, always seeking vengeance on those who did her harm or roused her to anger. Neighbours were all too willing to bear witness to her witchery, for she was feared throughout the burgh and nothing would please them more than to silence her forever. The charge was that she did wilfully conceive a cruel hatred and malice against Adam Clark, and for more than eighteen months sought to wreak her revenge by devilish means.

Extracts from the record of her trial show the extent of her mischief through incidents brought to light over the years.

November 1606: At about midnight Adam Clark and his wife were asleep. Apart from a serving woman in another bedroom, they were alone in the house. It was then when Isobel Grierson, in the likeness of a cat, entered the downstairs rooms 'with evil intent and crying out like a demon from Hell'. The household awakened, gripped with fear. Then the devil himself appeared as a black hairy man. When the serving woman ran in terror from her room, he seized her by the hair and dragged her about the house, tearing off her nightdress and throwing it on the fire.

January 1605: It is recorded that throughout that autumn and winter 'a devil in the likeness of a naked child' appeared each night at the house of William Burnett of Prestonpans, for whom Isobel Grierson 'conceived an evil will', perhaps because he slept with a widow remembered as Margaret Miller.

The apparition was said to stand before the fire, holding in its hand an enchanted wax doll. Often the doll was pierced with pins or the hand was held over its face; and the widow would awaken, fighting for breath, with stabbing pains in her chest.

On this particular night, the widow ran from her bed, gasping and clutching her breast, 'whereupon the naked child changed to the likeness of the said Isobel Grierson, pursuing the frightened woman about the house, wrestling her to the floor, and in a filthy and disreputable manner pissed upon the said Margaret Miller. Then the said William called out to Isobel by name, whereupon she vanished'.

The record tells that William Burnett wasted away of an unknown sickness, dying in pain and suffering.

October 1594: Isobel Grierson was accused of 'casting a sickness upon Robert Peddan, the said Robert remaining ill for one year and eighteen weeks, wasting and troubled with fainting fits . . .'

It was recalled that the victim owed the defendant a sum of 9s 4d, which he refused to pay. He was told that he should repent it. After long months of suffering he gave the woman ten shillings and begged that he be restored to health. The record tells that he recovered the next day.

January 1594: Neighbours told of a black cat, seen each night sitting on the windowsill of Robert Peddan's house. At that time he worked in the vats, brewing good Scottish ale.

Soon after the cat's nocturnal prowling, the taverns were deserted. The men who drank there described the ale from the casks as 'rotten, black, thick like gutter dirt, with filthy and pestilent odour'.

Hallowe'en 1605: The accused was said to have 'conceived deadly evil will, hatred and malice against Margaret Donaldson, spouse of said Robert Peddan'. She came to her in the silence of night, entering 'in devilish and unknown ways'. Finding the woman asleep in bed, she 'did throw her out headlong, tugging at the said Margaret's hair, and thereafter brought about a sorry physical and mental state in which every twenty-four hours or thereabout the woman did clutch at her head and breast with pains so severe that she became demented for more than an hour at a time . . .'

After much pleading that the spell be taken away, Isobel Grierson eventually relented. The women met and drank together, at which time Margaret was forgiven for causing offence and restored to normal health.

Absolution was short-lived, for it came to the ears of Isobel Grierson that the woman had slandered her in the company of others, denouncing her as a witch and a weaver of wicked spells. 'Whereupon the said Isobel did seek out Margaret Donaldson and spoke to her many horrible and devilish words, saying "Let the faggots of Hell light on you! May you seethe in Hell's cauldron!" Whereupon a sorry plight came to her again.'

At the trial the two women were brought face to face for examination in the presence of the Lord Justice, where Isobel Grierson was condemned as a sorceress – a user of charms and other devilish practices.

On 10th March, 1607, the evidence against the accused was overwhelming. All witnesses testified against her, and she was allowed to enter no defence. Found guilty of all charges, Isobel Grierson was taken to Castle Hill where she was strangled at the stake before her body was burned to ashes.

Witchery in Ayrshire

The following extract from the records of the Privy Council of Scotland illustrates man's inhumanity to his fellow beings during the sixteenth and seventeeth centuries – a time when witches were relentlessly pursued, their persecution was encouraged by ministers of the Church and supported by the fear and superstition of their followers.

> *December 1st in the year 1608:* The Earl of Mar declared to the Council that some women taken in Broughton as witches and being put to an assize and convicted, albeit they persevered constant in their denial to the end, yet were burned quick (alive) after such a cruel manner that some of them died in despair, renouncing and blaspheming God; and others, half-burned, brake out of the fire and were cast quick in it again till they were burned to the death.

The examination of Margaret Barclay at Irvine in Ayrshire in 1618 shows how harsh the cruelty of the Scots had become.

Margaret Barclay was the wife of Archibald Dein, a burgess of Irvine. She was a spirited young woman who, at the time, had quarrelled bitterly with her husband's brother and his wife after they had falsely accused her of thieving.

Her brother-in-law was the captain of a merchant ship. One day, when the vessel was getting under way for a voyage, she was seen at the quayside throwing burning coals into the water, and was heard to utter curses, invoking storms to rage and cast the ship upon the rocks.

Now there lived in Irvine a sinister character remembered as James Stewart, always suspicious and secretive in his ways. When the vessel did not return from its voyage on the appointed day, he was heard to tell of visions of a ship foundering at sea. Although he called to mind the curses of Margaret Barclay, his prophesy led to his arrest on suspicion of sorcery.

Under examination, he told the court that Margaret had asked that he show her some way of effecting the curse, and that when he had come to her house one night before the voyage had begun, he found her in the company of two other women. They were sitting together in the lamplight shaping images of a sailing craft and its master. Later that night the models were cast into the sea.

'I just told them the words to say,' the sorcerer recalled. 'Then the wind began to howl, and the water stirred. And a black dog appeared there among us!'

From those assembled in the court, he pointed out Margaret Barclay's accomplices. Although protesting her innocence, a woman called Isobel Insh was apprehended and locked up in the church belfry. Her eight-year-old daughter was then summoned to appear before the magistrates. Too young to understand the implications of her testimony, she told of two other women and a girl who were present at the water's edge, and of a 'black dog lighting the night with fire in its eyes'.

It is recorded that Isobel Insh fell from the belfry while attempting to escape, but both Margaret Barclay and James Stewart were indicted. Records further state that 'the said James Stewart was persuaded by the ministers to confess all and fall on the mercy of God who would loose him from the bonds of the Devil.' He was later found by the burgh officers hanging from the door of his prison cell, with a length of hemp from his bonnet tied to his throat, 'his knees being not half a span from the floor'.

Refusing to confess her witchery, Margaret Barclay was put to torture, by 'the onlaying of iron-gauds one by one to her bared legs as she was held in the stocks'. Only when her suffering became unbearable did she confess, and implicate her other accomplice, Isobel Crawford, who swore it was Margaret who had led her astray.

Archibald Dein acquired the services of a lawyer to defend his wife – a concession seldom permitted by the magistrates. She then retracted her confession, explaining that it had been forced from her by pain of torture. Her retraction was not accepted by the court who argued, with rare logic, that at the time of her confession she was experiencing no pain, for the manacles and iron-gauds were removed before her admission was given.

Proceedings were swiftly drawn to a close. Pronounced guilty, the accused was sentenced to be strangled at the stake before her body was burned. Her accomplice, Isobel Crawford, was similarly subjected to torture and suffered the same fate.

Seventeenth-century German instruments of torture
used at the Bamberg witch trials.

The White Witch of Perth

Long before the advance of medical science people looked to nature to provide remedies for fevers and phobias. Some were passed from one generation to the next, whilst others were born of superstition. The *Physicians of Myddfai* contains many recipes and remedies which seem strange in the twentieth century:

> A light dinner and less supper, sound sleep and a long life.

> If thou desireth to die, eat cabbage in August.

> Take the gall of a cat and hen's fat, mixing them together. Put this on your eyes and you will see things which are invisible to others.

In most towns and rural communities could be found the alchemist, the Knowing One – the white witches who practised a form of sorcery for the benefit of neighbours. But theirs was a dangerous calling, for those who one day implored wise men or old women to brew their herbs and weave their spells, the next may bear witness to their mischief as witches and clamour for their deaths.

The following are extracts from the examination of Isobel Haldane of Perth who appeared before the magistrates in the winter of 1623. Some accounts were described by witnesses, others were her own admission.

Her counsel was sought one day by the parents of infant Andrew Ducan, for the child had lain sick in his crib 'for two weeks together', growing weaker as each day passed. It was late at night when she tramped the moonlit glen, carrying a bucket of water scooped from a secluded loch. At the house where the child lay she fell to her knees, muttering blessings as she bathed the infant's head and limbs in the chill water. When the treatment was over she threw what remained in the bucket into the burn, but some was spilled on her way. With much care and consternation she wiped every drop from the path, for if anyone were to step in it or pass close by, then the sickness which had troubled the child would fall upon them.

On her travels through the streets of town one day Isobel Haldane met a young man who was visiting a carpenter. Soon his newborn son was to be delivered, and he was ordering a cradle in which the baby would lie.

Bearing witness before the magistrates, John Roch, the expectant father, and the carpenter, James Christie, testified that, 'the woman had come along, saying, "Be not in a hurry, for your wife will not bear a son until the moon is full again. And the child will never lie in its cradle, for it will be born, baptized, never suck; then die and will be taken away." This foretelling she had heard from an old man with a grey beard.'

Asked the name and whereabouts of this old man, Isobel Haldane explained how one night she was taken from her bed and led by the strains of faerie music to a faraway hillside. There she was lured into a cave that had no ending and where the sun never set. For several days she had stayed there, and an old man with a grey beard had been her guide. She had seen fairies dressed in sunset gold, flecked with silver. They had taught her how to look into the unknown, how to do good to poor folk, how to heal their sickness by bathing them in water from secret places.

It also transpired that the accused once sought out a woman who was working hard and cheerfully in the fields. She was told to prepare to meet her Maker, for before Fasting Eve the angel of death would come to take her away. And so it came about, because it had been foretold by the old man with the grey beard.

Another witness, a skinner of Perth named Patrick Ruthven, told how he had been bewitched by Margaret Hornscleugh and had asked Isobel to break the spell.

She would not accept the reward he offered, but went with him to his bed and there 'laid herself upon him full stretch, their bodies touching from head to foot while she muttered sighs and strange words he could not understand'. 'Many more times she came to my bed,' the skinner explained, 'until the spell all wore away.'

One night, the white witch trod the moonlit glen again, making her way stealthily to a holy well hidden in the braes. There she drew up a bucket of water to bathe John Gow's sick child. And when the simple baptism was over she returned to the secret place and left an article of the child's clothing in the still water of the well.

The remedy she effected with enchanted water, and sometimes a brew concocted from star-grass leaves, rarely failed to restore the victim to health. But on one occasion, it was learned, a child languished and died. It was not the charm or star-grass brew that caused the sufferer to waste away, the defendant explained. The child had been a changeling, over which the spell held no power.

In her attempt to defend herself by telling of her kindly deeds, Isobel Haldane had done more harm than good. Her recollections of that other world where the sun never sets, of shining elves, of the king of fairies with his silvery beard, served only to brand her as a 'weaver of charms', a 'disciple of the Evil One'.

Although associations with fairies played no part in the persecution of witches in England, it held a prominent role in Scotland where such Celtic beliefs were traditional. An Act of 1604 decreed that both white and black magic be viewed as equally evil. Those who wove spells only to ease the suffering of the unfortunate were themselves hounded and convicted by the very folk they wished to protect. This irony Isobel Haldane was to discover.

Witch Country

Essex, in East Anglia, has the distinction of having hanged more witches than any other English county. According to records it was there that the first and last public hangings for witchcraft took place – Agnes Waterhouse in 1566 and Alice Molland in 1684. During a period of eighty years spanning the sixteenth and seventeenth centuries almost a hundred supposed witches were sent to the gallows, including the execution of nineteen women in one day during the reign of their merciless witch-finder, Mathew Hopkins.

No old woman, infirm in body or mind, and with only a domestic pet to share her loneliness, was safe from his clutches. It was believed that witches were Satan's agents, dragging mankind to damnation, and that the variety of creatures that brought comfort to them were the Devil's familiars.

These relentless witch-hunts were born of fear, at a time when the Puritan community considered holy water and exorcism as Catholic superstition. Beliefs older than Christianity prevailed. Stone age pits, which were probably the remains of prehistoric flint mines, were said to be haunted by the terrible cries of tragedies of long ago. Stories were told of the Hounds of Odin or Black Shuck – dogs with luminous eyes and jaws dripping fire, that lurked among the hedgerows and graveyards.

Unlike witch trials in other parts of Europe, suspects in England were not charged with heresy. Theirs was the crime of maleficium – evil malice directed against the victim through the power of Satan.

In a Lancashire trial of 1612, Mother Demdike confessed that her maleficium was expressed by fashioning a clay likeness of her victim and piercing with a thorn that part of the image where injury was to be inflicted. 'When grave hurt was spelled,' she confessed, 'I let the doll smoulder in the fire, whereupon his body

Frontispiece of *Discoverie of Witches*
by Matthew Hopkins (Witch-Finder General), London, 1647.

withered away.' Isabel Gowdie, the Scottish witch, described how clay effigies of the wicked Laird's children were 'roasted over the flames little by little until they shrivelled with the heat and each child fair wasted away.'

In England it was forbidden to use scourging, thumbscrews, scalding water and similar implements of torture known on the Continent. But solitary confinement, starvation, cross-legged binding and long nights without sleep could be just as torturous.

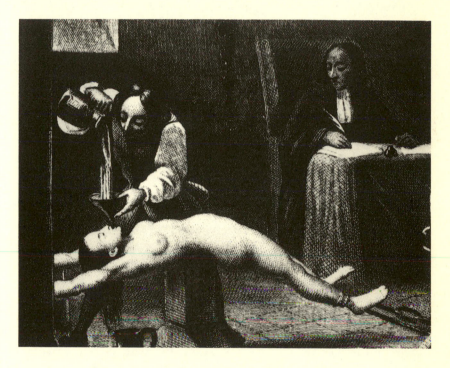

The water torture used to get witches to confess.
The victims stomach was forcibly filled with water until it became grossly distended. Then, if no confession was forthcoming,
the swollen stomach was beaten.

A statute against witchcraft, passed during the reign of Henry VIII in 1542, marks the beginning of persecution in England. It enacted that no one should invoke or conjure spirits . . . to injure another person or harm his belongings . . . to desecrate holy ground . . . Such mischief was adjudged felony, and offenders were to suffer pain of death, forfeiture of lands and chattels and the privilege of clergy and sanctuary.

Between 1566 and 1685 East Anglia, known then as the Witch Country, was gripped with hysteria. Based on hearsay evidence – sometimes the capricious stories of children – the accused were arrested and brought for examination. Trials were a mockery of justice. Courtrooms were besieged by mobs whose shouting and jeering made it impossible for the charges and testimony to be heard. In such an assembly, fraught with anger and bitterness, few magistrates had the courage to impose anything less than the death sentence.

The witch-hunts followed a pattern all too familiar: denunciation, interrogation in a cell, forced confession, then the hangman's noose. The most incredible evidence was readily accepted. There was an occasion during the trial of one Elizabeth Clarke when Mathew Hopkins swore on oath that there had come to visit the accused in her cell four of the Devil's familiars – a greyhound, a polecat, a white dog and a black imp. On another occasion, it was described how a male witch had flown over a church, clinging to the mane of a furry creature, and in so doing had caught his breeches on the steeple. The torn garment was produced as evidence and accepted by the magistrates.

A chronicle of bizarre trials is recorded in county archives. In 1579 Ellen Smith, whose mother had been hanged five years previously, was sent to the gallows for terrorizing a clergyman's daughter with a fierce dog, although the animal was never found nor seen by anyone other than the child. In the trials of 1589 unfortunate wretches accused of sorcery were hanged within two hours of their conviction. After days of privation one prisoner confessed to sending a ferret named Bid to torment a child who had taunted her. Eighty-year-old Joan Cunny and her daughter Alice admitted consorting with familiars. They had released two frogs called Jack and Jill into a farmer's byre to bewitch his cattle.

At St Osyth in 1921 a plough furrow revealed the bones of two female skeletons. Before burial, iron rivets had pierced the knees and elbows in an attempt, it is believed, to prevent their ghosts rising from the grave. Preserved now in a museum in Cornwall, the skeletons are thought to be the remains of Ursula Kemp and

Elizabeth Bennet, put to death in the witch purge of 1582, or of two witches hanged by Mathew Hopkins in 1645.

The first major trial for witchcraft was held at Chelmsford in 1566. It was typical of the primitive justice and trial procedures which prevailed in England at that time.

The Wiles of Satan

After days and nights without food and sleep and endless questioning, Elizabeth Francis, a native of the village of Hatfield Peverell in Essex, confessed to her inquisitors that as a young girl she had learned the wiles of witchcraft from her grandmother. She was to renounce God and follow the ways of the Devil.

'She gave me a spotted cat,' she explained, 'and said I was to call it by the name Satan after the master she served. I learned to understand the sounds it made, and read the glinting in its eyes.'

She treasured the gift, keeping the creature well fed and putting it to sleep on the blanket at the foot of her bed, not forgetting to keep the fur well groomed and to murmur softly to the cat as she did.

When Elizabeth grew to a young woman she tired of her life of poverty and loneliness, and wished for possessions of her own and a wealthy man for a husband. 'At once Satan knew my longing,' she said. 'And there came to the meadow a flock of sheep, all white and black. Their wool was soft as thistle-down, and always there was meat for the spit. They stayed for a time and presently they all wore away, and I never knew how.'

As her grandmother had directed, she rewarded the cat – her familiar spirit – by giving of her blood. She pierced the skin on her hand and put the blood into Satan's mouth. Then the creature lay down and purred contentedly. 'Look!' she said to the magistrates, holding out her hand. 'The marks will never go away.'

Elizabeth Francis was scorned by the wealthy man she sought for a husband. Seeking vengeance, she willed her familiar to waste the man's belongings. And when his wealth had dwindled away, she willed that his body be wasted too. So Satan went to him while he slept, nestling close and staring at him with fiery eyes.

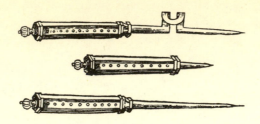

Prickers used by witch hunters to find the Devil's mark
on the skin with which Satan was supposed to brand his followers,
and which was insensible to pain.

'By and by the man took sick,' her inquisitors were told, 'and before winter came again he was dead.'

Later in her life Elizabeth took a husband. He treated her cruelly, sometimes beating her with a stick and cursing her slovenly ways. Once again she planned her revenge, and whispered her wishes to her old grannie's cat, who that night lay snug in her husband's boot. 'And when his foot touched where Satan had lied down,' her confession continued, 'he was taken with a lameness that never healed.'

The court determined that the cat was a devil, and learned that it had remained in Elizabeth's keeping for some fifteen years. 'Whenever it did my bidding,' she said, 'I gave it blood to drink, breaking my skin sometimes in one place, sometimes another. And these marks will never fade.'

It is difficult to understand why she should ever part with the creature that helped with her witchery and wicked schemes. Perhaps she was stricken with remorse or began to fear its mystic powers. Whatever the reason, records tell that Elizabeth grew weary of Satan and gave it to Mother Waterhouse, a poor woman of the neighbourhood. It was taken along, wrapped in her apron. She told the woman that the cat would bring about her wishes for as long as she lived. She had only to feed it well and reward it from time to time with a little of her blood, and to call its name Satan. Mother Waterhouse chuckled with glee and, muttering her gratitude, she took from the oven a freshly baked cake.

Perhaps it was because Elizabeth Francis had voluntarily forsaken her ways of wickedness that the court was moved to leniency. She was sent to prison for twelve months. But later she returned to her old ways of witchery. Some thirteen years passed before she was once more charged with causing personal injury to others by devilish wiles, and she was sent to the scaffold in 1579.

Before the court at Chelmsford in 1566 appeared the widow Agnes Waterhouse, a wizened woman with bent shoulders and a pock-marked face. After days of hunger and solitary confinement her spirit was broken and she confessed to many offences. Just as Elizabeth Francis had done, she had willed her cat, Satan, to bring mischief to her neighbours and their belongings.

When Father Kersey had accused her of stealing, she 'went about his house one night while the moon was hid, and set Satan free in his hog pen'. When morning came three hogs were dead, and the cat was back home sleeping in a basket. For serving her well she rewarded her familiar by scratching deep into her cheek and giving it a trickle of blood to drink.

'After a squabble with Widow Goodday,' she further confessed, 'I wished to Satan that her cow be drowned and her geese mauled. And the next day the beast was found all swelled and floating in the river. And the geese were all squandered about in the coop, with bloody beaks and feathers.' Satan, she remembered, had returned home at dawn and stretched out on the windowsill, napping in the morning sun. She rewarded her pet as before, feeding it with blood drained from her cheek, 'like old Grannie Eve had shown to her granddaughter, and Elizabeth had showed to me'.

Widow Waterhouse raised her hand to her face and touched the sores still festering there.

Out of spite for others she had willed Satan spoil the brewing of hops, turn butter sour in the churn, and wither crops in the field. Most of this evidence was given by a young maid and accepted as fact by the magistrates.

Another neighbour and his wife drove her from their door when she came begging. So she vowed that ill should befall them both. And before many days had passed they died of the bloody flux.

As her confession unfolded, she told how she had lived unquiet-ly with her husband, and how Satan had helped her waste away his spirit and send him to his grave. Since that time, some nine years past, she had lived in poverty as a widow. Her cat, with baleful eyes and spotted fur was, in truth, the Devil incarnate, she owned.

It was Satan who foretold her fate. One day as she wandered on her way to the nearby village of Braxted her familiar urged that she make haste, for trouble was soon to befall her, and that she was to die by fire or choking.

Apart from her confession and the evidence of a young maid, Agnes Waterhouse's doom was sealed when it was discovered that she could recite her prayers only in Latin – a sorry indictment in Protestant England. She was sent to the gallows at Chelmsford soon after her trial, and it is likely that she has the distinction of being the first woman in England to be hanged for witchcraft.

The third defendant appearing before the court was Joan Waterhouse, granddaughter of Agnes. A frightened girl, barely past her eighteenth birthday, she was accused of bewitching the twelve-year-old daughter of a local gentleman.

The only testimony offered in evidence was that of the victim herself who could name no witness to the alleged assault, during which a fierce, spotted animal so terrorized her that she became partially paralysed, never to regain the use of her limbs on the right side of her body.

'It growled and crouched down low ready to spring at my throat,' she explained, 'all the time staring at me with lighted eyes!'

In her defence, Joan told how she had gone to the girl's home, begging for a crust of bread and cheese. 'I was driven off without food or pity,' she said tearfully, 'although they had more than enough to eat. Stones and curses were throwed after me as I ran away.'

Candidly, the accused admitted that for a time she had harboured wicked thoughts and longed for revenge. Sometimes, she recalled, her grandmother had muttered strange spells and kept company with a cat called Satan. But she had taken little part in such witchery, for she feared the animal's sharp claws and smouldering eyes, and had no wish to give her blood and soul to the Devil.

When she had returned to her cottage that day, hungry and trembling with anger, she sat brooding before the fire. In the hearth beside her, Satan the cat lay sleeping.

The girl had muttered to herself about the family who had so cruelly driven her away, and about how she wished that some misfortune should befall them. She hadn't noticed the cat open its eyes and creep away from the hearth, not returning until dusk.

Considering how often in subsequent trials suspects were convicted on the unsupported evidence of children, Joan Waterhouse was lucky to be acquitted. She was subjected to the indignity of being stripped of all her clothes before the court so that her body could be examined for witch marks.

To Catch the Devil

From the neighbouring county of Suffolk comes the story of Amy Duny, a native of Lowestoft who, in the winter of 1664, was put on trial at Bury St Edmunds, charged with sorcery and bewitching a child. From the outset she protested her innocence, but was damned by flimsy evidence and the credulity of the magistrates.

That winter Amy had worked at the home of a Mrs Durent, helping about the house and watching over her young daughter. There were times when she sat at the child's bedside, telling stories or singing lullabies in the candlelight.

Then, one night, the girl cried out in her sleep and awakened from a fearful dream. In the weeks that followed, the nightmares continued, until her eyes grew heavy from lack of sleep, and the colour was drained from her cheeks. She began to dread the dark, and often she would sit for longer than an hour staring into the fire, oblivious of everything around her.

At that time there lived in a village not far away a Knowing One who was believed to understand the mystery of spells, and to prescribe remedies which would dispel them. So to the house of the wise man went the mother, leading the child by the hand.

'The young one is clearly bewitched,' the man declared. 'Some agent of the Devil has entered your house and put her under a spell.'

His antidote was as strange as the affliction that had come upon the girl. The mother was told to wrap the child in a blanket, and while the blanket was still warm with the heat of her body, she was to drape it beneath the chimney, where it was to remain through the hours of darkness. 'The Evil One takes on several mantles,' he advised, 'and whatever creature, large or small, is drawn therein must be thrown upon the fire. Then the spell will be broken and the child will be haunted no longer.'

Returning home, the mother did as the wise man prescribed, wrapping her daughter's naked body in a freshly laundered blanket which was then hung about the irons under the chimney. That night she lay beside the child, keeping watch over her while she slept.

At first light the woman groped her way to the hearth, for the room was clouded in smoke. There she gathered together the corners of the blanket and was startled to discover that some creature was stirring in its folds. It then scratched and wriggled furiously in an effort to escape. In fright she flung the blanket and whatever it contained into the grate. It smouldered in the embers, and presently a large, black rat emerged, squealing with pain.

Some time later, Amy Duny was seen to have blisters on her face and hands, as though she had been scalded.

No one asked the cause of her injury, nor listened to her explanation. The magistrates saw no reason other than to believe the story told by Mrs Durent, which was accepted as the whole truth.

On 13th March, 1664, Amy Duny was found guilty as charged. Three days later, still protesting her innocence, she was hanged at Bury St Edmunds.

May God Forgive Them

After the reign of Mathew Hopkins, East Anglia's witch-finder, the witch-hunts and injustice continued and in the years that followed, the county was the scene of many more executions.

One case involved Deborah and Elizabeth Pacy, aged nine and eleven years. It is said that while their testimony was heard during a trial at Bury St Edmunds in 1662, the accused could offer no evidence in her own defence. A spinster, living alone in an isolated cottage, she could call on no one to speak on her behalf. Throughout her examination she sat with her head lowered and was heard

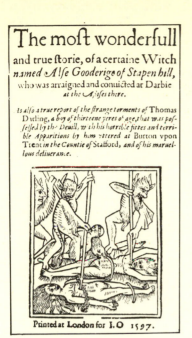

The most wonderfull and true storie, of a certaine Witch named Alse Gooderige of Stapen hill, who was arraigned and conuicted at Darbie at the Assises there.

Is also a true report of the strange torments of Thomas Darling, a boy of thirteene yeres of age, that was possessed by the Deuill, with his horrible fittes and terrible Apparitions by him vttered at Burton vpon Trent in the Countie of Stafford, and of his maruellous deliuerance.

Printed at London for I. O 1597.

The Apprehension and confession of three notorious Witches. Arreigned and by Iustice condemned and executed at Chelmes-forde, in the Countye of Essex, the 5. day of Iulye, last past. 1589.

With the manner of their diuelish practices and keeping of their spirits, whose fourmes are heerein truelye proportioned.

IOAN PRENTIS & hir Bid

JACK

Title page from an English book on witches dated 1597.

Title page of a book about three notorious witches who were hanged at Chelmsford, Essex in 1589.

to mutter, 'I know nothing of their trouble. May God forgive them.'

It was alleged that the children were stricken with a strange sickness. Sometimes, for hours on end, their legs would be numbed so that they could neither walk nor stand upon them. They would fall into mysterious fits, their heads and limbs twitching, and froth bubbling at their mouths. At other times their bodies became so tender that they cried out at the slightest touch.

'It was only after the woman cast her evil eye on us that we were troubled,' the children told the court. 'She is a witch!' they cried, pointing an accusing finger.

It was recorded that once in a while, as they lay awake in bed, they felt a presence in their room. The candle flame flickered, and they wrapped the blanket tightly around their shoulders when the room suddenly became cold.

In his deposition, a physician described how the children were struck dumb with fright. 'They would never utter a word for days together,' he said. 'Sometimes they coughed and vomited, bringing up much blood and phlegm, and with it crooked pins that scratched their throats.'

Several of these pins were shown as evidence. There was no medical explanation for the children's odd symptoms – no mention of fever, epilepsy, hysteria. It was held that none of these was the cause of their sickness; nor were the symptoms attributed to the imagination and nightmares. The examiners chose to believe that the Devil had come to visit through the spells of his agents.

During these trials of 1662 many other innocent people, mostly defenceless women of lowly birth, were to suffer as a result of hysterical, unsupported condemnation by children. It is argued that it set the pattern for the witchcraft delusion in Salem, New England.

The trials at Bury St Edmunds constituted the last major persecution in England. Thereafter, executions were rare. Superstition faded with the years, to be replaced with tolerance and understanding. At Exeter, in 1684, a woman named Alice Holland was the last person in England to be convicted and hanged for witchcraft.

White Witches of the East

There are few people who remember the name Cunning Murrell, for his house has long since fallen to ruin and he was buried in Hadleigh churchyard in an unmarked grave more than a century ago.

Born the seventh son of a seventh son, he was known throughout the county of Essex as a magician who could dispel the Devil's curses and exorcize evil spirits. From the far corners of the county, folk came to seek his counsel and ask him to unravel spells of witchery.

Whenever the night sky was clear he would stare at the stars and read prophesies there. It is said that even those too distant to show their light did not escape his gaze. Most precious of his possessions was a looking-glass which, like the Celtic *Pwll Cyfareddol* (Pool of

Magic), reflected secrets hidden in the future. He also had a copper talisman that lost its lustre when untrue stories were told.

The counter-spells of Cunning Murrell were the most weird imaginable – the rarest herbs and incantations galore. Best remembered and most potent was his 'witch's brew', a small container of iron which sealed a concoction of peculiar ingredients.

One day a mother and her young daughter came to his house, asking that he unbind a spell that had been cast upon the child by a gipsy. He was told that at times the girl would crawl about on hands and knees and howl like a wolf.

Cunning Murrell first stared into the victim's eyes and then into his looking-glass. 'The child is cursed,' he decided. He held his looking-glass close to the light. 'I see here her tormentor, hunched in a caravan, chuckling at the girl's misfortune.'

Then he prepared the recipe for his counter-spell. Into his small iron casket he put a lock of the girl's hair, clippings from her finger nails and a drop of her blood, pricked from the end of her finger, then a trickle more drawn from a cross scratched on her forehead. 'When the casket is held over the fire,' he told them, 'the witch will be racked with pain until the curse is withdrawn.'

A few nights later, when the moon was bright, the spell breaker placed his brew upon his fire. It simmered there for a time. Then came a sizzling and a spluttering until the casket burst open, scattering its contents among the flames.

The following morning, so the story is told, the charred body of a woman was found lying in a country lane. No one could imagine how she met her end. But the girl who came to seek the help of Cunning Murrell was troubled no more.

✳   ✳   ✳

In the village of Willingham, a lonely corner of Cambridgeshire, there once lived a Knowing One whose spells were cast only to drive away the mischief of black magic. He concocted potions to heal the sick, bring love to the sad at heart, and to unravel mysteries. He could frighten away poltergeists, exorcize ghosts, and bring fertility to those who were barren. Nothing lay beyond his skill.

One day a young widow came to him and told of a man who

came to her window after dark to peer into her room. Even when the curtains were tightly drawn, there was always a chink left bare. There he would linger for an hour or more, tapping on the window pane, calling her name affectionately. When evening drew on she would bolt the door and huddle in a corner hidden from his gaze. Sometimes she would blow out the lamp and sit in the firelight, with only her cat to keep her company. She never dared undress or go to her bed until long after all was quiet outside.

The prowler, she suspected, was Jabez Few, shunned by all the young women of the village as a lecher, who gained his wicked ways by witchcraft. It was known that in his house he kept a nest of white mice – a favour from the Devil to help him with romantic conquests.

'It will soon be time for bed, my love,' she would hear him call from outside the window. 'Take off your clothes. I can barely see you in the firelight. Sarah, Sar—ah! If it's cold beneath the blankets you have only to unfasten the bolt . . .'

'It's likely his way of winning your attention,' the Knowing One smiled, mindful of her pretty face and lithe figure.

The more the widow hid from Jabez Few, the more persuasive and persistent he became. Not a night passed by without his presence at the window. With the curtains closed and the lamp turned low, she could feel his eyes looking in at her. Long after bedtime she would hear him skulk away, muttering curses. Once he pounded on her door until the bolt rattled and the timbers shook. But not once did she call back.

Whenever Sarah went shopping in the village and Jabez Few was seen approaching, she crossed to the other side of the street, with never a glance of encouragement. The more she ignored him the more bitter he became.

One night he was not alone when he came to her cottage window, for a nest of mice wriggled in his pocket. As usual his tapping outside and calling her name brought no response. The lamp went out, and through a chink in the curtains he saw only the fluttering of flames around the hearth.

'After a while I heard him at the threshold,' the widow explained to the Knowing One. 'Then from under the door little creatures came scampering in, and the cat's eyes shone bright as it pounced on them.'

A fearful struggle ensued. Shadows moved swiftly about the room. There was a growling and a snarling and shrieks of pain, as when a fox is cornered by the hounds. The frightened widow could only listen and wonder.

When, at last, the confusion died down and the lamp was lit, there was no sign of Jabez Few's mice. But the cat, torn and bleeding, was clinging terrified to the banister rail.

There were times, usually in the quiet of night, when the creatures were heard stirring in the cottage: soft footfalls, a weird, stifled lowing – quite unlike the sound of mice. When this presence was felt, the widow would stay curled in her bed, too frightened to move. And the cat would nestle in the crook of her knees, its ears erect.

Smearing a witch with flying ointment.

With a sigh and a frown, the Knowing One of Willingham rummaged through his chest of herbs and bones and shrivelled blossoms, all ingredients for his magic potions. From these he made his selection and put the mixture in a stone jar. Then together they set off for the widow's cottage. There the Knowing One gathered sprinkles of earth from beneath the window where the tormentor had trod, adding them to his recipe.

As nightfall approached, the stone jar was laid on the fire. While it boiled they stood watching at the window. Presently they caught sight of Jabez Few. Pale as death and writhing with pain, he came to the cottage door. There he whistled aloud and called strange names until his nest of mice were heard scurrying from the skirtings.

From that day on, the widow Sarah was left in peace. No one knows whatever became of her, nor of the Knowing One of Willingham. But it is recorded that Jabez Few lies buried in the local cemetery. It is said that after his death the mice lived on, swarming about his house. Neither traps nor poison could stop their multiplying.

There they remained until a nephew diverted a stream to run through the garden. Then they vanished as though some Pied Piper had spirited them away.

Meon Hill

Standing on the border between Warwick and Gloucestershire, Meon Hill is the last outpost of the Cotswolds. From its summit it commands a view of several English counties and is exposed to wind and rain. Of limestone outlier with a Marlstone cap, it is claimed by geologists that the hill was formed during the Jurassic period. But mythology tells how the Devil, enraged at the later foundation of the Christian abbey at Evesham, determined to bury forever the house of God beneath a huge mound of earth. This he tore from the ground and hurled in the direction of the abbey. However, to prevent such sacrilege, St Egwin intercepted the missile's trajectory and it fell instead on the barren land where it stands today as Meon Hill.

There is evidence to suggest a pre-Christian existence on the hill – an iron-age fort with ditches and ramparts, deposits of gold and pottery dating from the first century BC and ruins of a Roman villa on the northern shoulder. For countless centuries the hill has overlooked the green fields and quiet hamlets of the English countryside.

Long ago, wakes and sabbats were common occurrences on its desolate slopes. More recently, a series of macabre events have been reported there – incidents which always will remain a mystery.

Winter 1875: At nearby Long Compton the body of an old woman, Ann Turner, was discovered with a pitchfork piercing her throat and pinning her to the ground. Across her face and chest was slashed the sign of the cross. James Heywood, a young farmworker, had long suspected the woman of being a witch.

'It's she who brings the floods and drought,' he once accused. 'Her spells withered the crops in the field. Her curse drove my father to an early grave!'

Often he had protested that only the spilling of her blood would take away the old woman's evil powers. And so when Ann Turner's body was discovered suspicion was aroused and the farmhand was charged with her murder. During his trial at Warwick Assizes he asked that the victim be weighed against the Holy Bible – a rare custom prevalent in past centuries.

For his crime James Heywood was convicted and sentenced to life imprisonment. But there were many among the inhabitants of Long Compton and surrounding villages who were never convinced of his guilt. Seventy years were to pass before memories of the incident were awakened.

Autumn 1885: It was dusk when Charles Walton, a fourteen-year-old shepherd boy, was returning home after a day in the hills. The evening was still. Passing through a copse, he heard footsteps rustling among the fallen leaves.

Turning to look over his shoulder, he saw a black dog following him which he later described to his family as a fierce-looking animal with a face resembling that of a bull terrier. It neither growled nor barked, but just stared at him with eyes that smouldered like burning coals.

Each evening as he made his way home the beast followed, sometimes emerging from among the trees, at other times trotting behind along the hillside paths. It made no sound and always vanished as mysteriously as it had appeared. When he described how one evening the apparition had transformed into the shape of a woman wearing a black cloak his story was received with chuckles of derision.

Although it was commonly believed that the appearance of a spectral black dog foreshadowed misfortune and bereavement, little was thought of the shepherd boy's tales until a day when news was heard of his younger sister's tragic death.

Whether from grief at his loss or fear of the unknown, from that time on the boy spent most of his days alone, suspicious of all strangers. No one, except perhaps the members of his family, was at ease in his company, for it was believed that the Devil had set his mark on him.

Winter 1945: Sixty years passed by. Charles Walton, now an old man, set out one morning with billhook and pitchfork to do some hedging in a field on Meon Hill. It was the last time he was to leave his cottage and the niece with whom he lived.

Following a search that evening his mutilated body was found in the field where he had been working. The *Stratford Herald* of 15th February described how the front of his clothing had been torn away and wounds in the form of a cross were slashed across his heart. A two-pronged pitchfork pierced his throat and had been plunged deep into the ground, holding his head fast. Cuts on his arms and hands indicated that the victim had put up a fearful struggle.

The local police, assisted by an inspector from Scotland Yard, regarded the murder as the work of some crazed person, for there was no apparent motive. It was considered unlikely that the old man should be brutally attacked for a cheap pocket watch – his only missing possession.

One suspect who had been seen near the scene of the crime was questioned by the police. He was an Italian from a Prisoner of War camp at Long Marston. Blood-stained clothing was found hidden at his camp. But forensic examination proved that the Italian's clothes were soiled by rabbit's blood, and that his misdemeanour was only poaching.

The killing of Charles Walton puzzled the inspector, who spent many hours searching for clues at the scene of the attack and in the near vicinity. By strange coincidence he told of the appearance of a large black dog on several occasions while he was alone on Meon Hill. Villagers were reluctant to volunteer any information which might shed light on the mystery. They muttered only that a ghostly dog was said to haunt the hill, and that from time to time strange happenings were known, especially after dark. Shadowy figures were seen and fearful noises heard.

As investigation continued, more sinister motives were uncovered. From past records a comparison was drawn with the murder of an old woman at Long Compton in 1875. Dr Margaret Murray, the distinguished Professor of Egyptology, was consulted. Her research showed that the date of Charles Walton's killing, calculated by the old calendar, coincided with the day when Druids performed rites of human sacrifice to ensure the fertility of their fields. She suggested it was likely a pitchfork had been used to force back the head of the victim so that blood could more easily flow to the soil. There was also an ancient belief that the shedding of a witch's blood exorcized evil spells.

Apart from the company of his niece, Charles Walton had led a solitary life, searching more into the secrets of nature than for the companionship of farmers and shepherds who lived around him. Villagers recalled that he was a vindictive old man, sometimes harnessing toads, yoked with reeds and pieces of ram's horn. These he willed to cross fields, blighting crops and harbouring thistles and briers. They remembered, too, that hidden at the back of his pocket watch he kept a 'witch's mirror' – a black stone, polished in a mountain stream.

Among the villages in the shadow of Meon Hill, where even today a belief in witchcraft is not dead, the inhabitants have learned to accept that the murder of Charles Walton was either a ritual killing or an act of vengeance.

It was not until the summer of 1960, when outbuildings behind his cottage were demolished, that the old man's pocket watch was discovered. But the sliver of polished stone said to have been concealed in its cavity – his witch's looking-glass – the crystal used for weaving spells or seeing into the future was never found.

Was this the talisman for which he was slain? Was the old man's killer some crazed wanton? Or was the motive revenge for an act of witchery? If the true identity of the culprit was known, no one ever dared tell and the mystery will forever remain unsolved.

The Rollright Stones

The Cotswold country, with its wide sweeps of upland and open spaces interspersed with cottages and farmhouses of ancient weathered stone, abounds in stories of witchcraft. It is said of some villages that there were enough witches to pull a wagon-load of hay up Long Compton hill.

The Rollright Stones, Oxfordshire.

At the top of the hill, hidden from the main road, stand the Rollright Stones, a prehistoric circle dating back before 1500 BC, and a favourite meeting place for witches in years gone by.

Legend tells how once an invading king and his retainers stood on a ridge which commands a view of two counties. There they

121

were confronted by a witch of Shipton-under-Wychwood. Learning of their intent, she cast a spell under which the invaders were turned to stone – the Kingstone below the crest of the mound, and his men in a circle behind him. Farther to the east stand a group of stones known as the Whispering Knights, traitors plotting the downfall of their leader.

In his *Folklore and Superstitions in Shakespeare's Land*, Harvey Bloom describes incidents which illustrate the mystery of the place.

For example, each evening farmers closed their gates so that the cattle would not stray. But even though they were securely fastened with stout ropes and padlocks, when morning came the gates were found to be wide open.

Another farmer remembered how once his father had attempted to bridge a stream on his land. With iron bars and a team of oxen he dislodged one of the stones. But though his beasts laboured all day long to drag it down the slope of the hill their task was abandoned at nightfall, with the team exhausted and the stone moved barely half a furlong from the hilltop.

It is hardly credible that he should strive to return the stone to its original place. But this he did the following morning, perhaps because of an unusual thunderstorm that came with the dusk, or weird cries that haunted him through the night.

As he tugged on the reins the oxen refused to move from the byre. They dug their hoofs into the ground and lowed pitifully, as though terrified of some alien presence. Unable to stir the beasts, the farmer led his shire-horse instead up the hillside, and was amazed to discover the ease with which the animal was able to pull the stone to the summit.

It is not everyone living in England's heartland who regards witchcraft as black art belonging to centuries past. Even today, homes and taverns have lines drawn around the hearth and along the edge of the floorboards to keep out dark spirits. Beyond these marks witches and demons dare not steal from the chimney or ascend from the darkness of the ground.

The mystery which for thousands of years has surrounded the Rollright Stones persists in the twentieth century.

The story is told of a young wife who lived in the village of

Snowshill some fifty years ago. Although she was blessed with good health and a happy marriage, above all else she longed for a child of her own. As the years passed, her longing grew, and loneliness made her sad.

At that time there lived in the village a kindly old widow who, through her life, had uncovered many of nature's secrets. From reading patterns in the sky and observing the ways of wild creatures of the countryside she foretold the unrelenting snow-storm of 1881. With her herbal remedies she cured villagers stricken with fever. And once, it was whispered, she broke a spell cast on a family by a beggar from Winchcombe.

So one day, while her husband was working in the fields, the young wife, afraid that she would remain always barren, knocked on the widow's door and told of her troubles.

'Save your tears,' the old widow told her when she saw her so upset. 'Some day there'll be many you'll shed for your young ones, for they will bring you happiness and heartache.'

For a long time they sat together at the fireside, the young wife dreaming, the old woman remembering. And when at last they parted, the young wife's tears were gone and her heart was lighter, for in her apron pocket she carried a special brew of plants picked from the hills and meadows, and a talisman to lay under her pillow.

The autumn wore on and winter came, and still she remained infertile. Neither potion nor charm had fulfilled her longing. She hid the talisman among the sheets whenever she and her husband were roused to passion; she stirred drops of the potion into his drink. But still no seed bore fruit.

She returned to the widow's cottage, feeling more disappointed than the time before. And the kindly old soul shared her anxiety. Perhaps it was never meant to be, she supposed. Perhaps the young wife of Snowshill would always be childless. And then her eyes brightened when she remembered a remedy never known to fail.

'Come again after nightfall,' she urged. 'Steal away while your husband sleeps.' She drew close and whispered. 'Remember to leave long before the clock strikes twelve, and tell no one of our meeting.'

Once more the young wife's heart beat faster as she hurried home before darkness fell. When supper was over her husband was soon asleep, worn out after toiling in the fields. No one saw her as she passed through the shadows of the country lane and crossed the meadow to the old widow's cottage.

As they trudged up Long Compton hill the young wife tingled with excitement. But in answer to all her eager questions the widow placed a finger to her lips. 'Not a sound!' she warned breathlessly. 'All will be well. You'll see.'

They approached the hilltop from the east, and when they reached the summit the Whispering Knights stood black against the sky. The widow spoke in a hushed voice, pointing to the stone sentinels.

'The Knights tell what is hidden in the future, if your ears are sharp enough to hear their whispering.'

'Will they look into the future and know if I shall be blessed?' The young wife's voice trailed away as her companion held out a hand to silence her.

'Listen!' she breathed. 'Not a sound. The Knights can read what's in your thoughts.'

Together they stood there in the moonlight, listening, listening. The Whispering Knights were stark and silent as tombstones. Minutes passed, but not a sound did they hear. They crept nearer, until the dark shapes loomed large above them. And then . . . Could it have been the wind sighing, or the voices of spirits whispering? 'A son . . . son . . . son!' they seemed to say.

The young wife gasped with wonder. But their mission was not yet over. Beyond the Whispering Knights they went, until they came to the petrified king and his retainers. There, as the hour of midnight approached, the young wife was told to take off her clothes and stand naked against the Kingstone. She did as she was instructed, pressing her body so close that her lips and breasts and thighs were chilled by its touch. While the chiming of the churchyard clock drifted from the village beyond, she stood pressed against the Kingstone in silent homage, murmuring her heartfelt desire.

The old widow smiled in satisfaction. It was a ritual that always came to pass – a promise foretold by the Whispering Knights.

No one will ever know whether that night the Rollright Stones changed the young wife's destiny. But in the years to come she was blessed with grandchildren to comfort her in her old age – all born of her three sons.

Mystery at Hagley Wood

Hagley Wood lies about half-a-mile from the road running from Kidderminster to Birmingham. It is a quiet spot, situated on the estate of Lord Cobham of Hagley Hall, and is well known as a haunt for lovers. Local historians tell us that in years gone by witch covens and Devil worshippers met there in the shadows of the Clent Hills.

Witches dancing, from *The Witch of the Woodlands*.

It was dusk one summer's evening when a gardener on the estate was making his way home along the woodland paths, his work done, and his supper awaiting him. He did not know that the first day of August coincided with the festival of Lammas – the witches' eve of *Lugnasadh* in the old Celtic calendar.

As he was passing through the heart of the woods he was startled to hear a scream coming from nearby. It silenced the birds and prompted him to stop in his tracks, listening and looking all around. Moments later it came again – the shrill cry of someone in terror.

Although he searched among the trees he saw no one. For many minutes more he waited there, and then continued on his journey, treading more gingerly along the beaten track. But now the woods were quiet again.

That night he reported the incident to friends at the local tavern, and later he led a band of villagers to the place where the screaming was heard, because that morning a young woman from Halesowen had set out from home and had not returned by nightfall. No clue pointed to the young woman's whereabouts, and they heard nothing more alarming than the cry of a screech-owl.

Throughout the following day neighbours continued the search, retracing the gardener's steps, combing the woods from edge to edge. But, although the story was reported to the local magistrates and further search parties were organized, the missing woman was never found. Two summers passed and her disappearance remained a mystery.

Then one afternoon, while walking in the woods, two young girls from the village stopped to rest beneath a wych-elm. Among the fallen leaves they found what at first they took to be an eagle's talon. However, on closer inspection, they discovered to their horror that it was the bones of a hand with two middle fingers broken away.

As they searched around, another gruesome sight was revealed. In the hollow trunk of the tree they found a human skeleton wedged behind the bark and crudely concealed among a heap of withered leaves and bracken. The arms were twisted grotesquely upwards and backwards over the skull, and decayed fragments of clothing were still attached to the bones.

The girls ran screaming from the woods, not suspecting that

they might have unearthed a victim of witches and Devil worshippers, for it was believed that a human hand was much coveted by servants of Satan.*

This grisly charm, often hacked from the corpse of a hanged murderer as he wasted on the gibbet, was used to point out the whereabouts of buried treasure or mortal enemies, and sometimes to ward off offending spirits.

That night the lamps were burning long after dark, and neighbours gathered together, wondering who the culprit might be. Among them, they knew, was one whose dark deed had been brought to light, whose well-kept secret had been unveiled.

At each of the girls' doorways the following morning was found a circle of yew twigs and gravestone chippings. And each knew well how to read this warning sign – to speak no more of what they had discovered in the woods, or their tongues would be silenced forever.

---

* Long ago, tales of the 'Magic Hand', or 'Hand of Glory', were well known throughout Europe, Africa and the voodoo lands of the West Indies.

'The Devil he flung her on a horse,
And he leapt up before.'

The Devil's Due

Appearing in old chronicles is the following poem by Robert Southey, based on a tale from the ninth century. It describes how a witch, at the end of her days, was taken away by her Master, the Devil.

The raven croak'd as she sate at her meal,
    And the old woman knew what he said.
And she grew pale at the raven's tale,
    And sickened went to her bed.

'I have 'nointed myself with infant's fat.
    The fiends have been my slaves.
From sleeping babes I have sucked the breath;
    And breaking by charms the sleep of death
I have called the dead from their graves.

'And the Devil will fetch me now in fire,
    My witchcraft to atone;
And I who have troubled the dead man's grave
    Shall never rest in my own.'

They blest the old woman's winding sheet
    With rites and prayers that were due.
With holy water they sprinkled her shroud,
    And they sprinkled her coffin too.

And in he came with eyes of flame –
    The Devil to fetch the dead.
And all the church with his presence glow'd
    Like a fiery furnace red.

He laid his hands on the iron chains;
    And like flax they moulder'd asunder.

And the coffin lid which was barr'd so firm
   He burst with his voice of thunder.

And he bade the old woman of Berkeley rise
   And come with her master away.
A cold sweat started on that cold corpse,
   At the voice she was forced to obey.

The Devil he flung her on a horse,
   And he leapt up before.
And away like the lightning's speed they went;
   And she was seen no more.

ROBERT SOUTHEY, 1774–1843

The Sorceress

In the county of Wiltshire the story is remembered of Dr Lamb, revered as an alchemist and as a physician to those of noble birth. Everyone wondered at the medicines he prescribed.

'Sickness comes furtively to torment us,' was his philosophy. 'It is like the mist stealing over the plains. But always the remedy is hidden somewhere nearby – in the roots and leaves and berries of nature's garden. For those who seek there are plants for every ill.'

For a long time he prospered as a healer, a brewer of rare potions. Then came the time when his thoughts turned to the art of divination – the discovery of the unknown by delving into the supernatural. He was known to keep company with witches, to invoke devils, and to pay homage to the spirits of darkness. Fearful of his new-found power and ungodly ways, villagers were roused to anger, which led to his tragic end.

Suspecting that he had brought upon them a season of misfortune – floods at harvest time, sickness among the cattle, children ailing with infectious diseases; and believing that the devils he had summoned lay at the heart of this mischief, the doctor was driven from his house and chased through the streets. At the cross of St Paul he was cornered and stoned to death.

But the mysterious paths of Dr Lamb's journey into the unknown were not hidden forever, for he had taken as his mistress a young woman, Anne Bodenham. With her, he had shared the secrets of alchemy and divination. And so a practice carried down from the Dark Ages, when primitive tribes learned to foretell future events by studying the entrails of animals, continued to flourish in the seventeenth century. His apprentice became the sorceress, entrusted with the art of fire gazing, interpreting dreams and nocturnal visions, with conjured spirits to mark the way into the unknown.

As the years passed, Anne Bodenham prospered by virtue of the

Anne Bodenham divining the future
with a brazier of burning coals and dancing spirits.

fears and superstition of those who were artless and easily led. Many was the time, long after neighbours had gone to their beds, when a lamplight shone in her window. It was then that that the curious, the covetous and the tormented came to seek her counsel.

One night there came to her door a young maid with tears glistening in her eyes. She was broken-hearted because her lover had forsaken her.

'I long for him although he uses me cruelly,' she sighed. And might there not be some spell with which to win his love and charm him back again, she wondered.

As they sat together, the sorceress gazed into the fire: at the flames flickering in the grate and wisps of smoke curling up the chimney. For a long time she gazed in silence.

'Your lover is a philanderer,' she said at length. 'His heart is cold and belongs to no one.' Then she consulted her Book of Shadows and found there a fitting prescription.

While the moon was on the wane the forsaken maid was to search among the waste ground. There she would find a plant with leaves like an eagle's feathers, flowers with purple veins, and petals as pale as death. She was to pluck a sprig of the henbane and crush it to a meagre philtre, for one drop of its juice would turn a beastly man to love.

'If then his heart should not melt,' the sorceress warned, 'he has no love for anyone, and better that he go to an early grave!'

The maid gasped with wonder, but dared not interrupt.

'Go then to the cross roads, and search the ground beneath the gibbet for a plant in the shape of a dancing man, with roots like cloven hoofs that shriek when they are plucked. Soak this in the cup of your faithless lover, for the mandrake will silence man or rabid beast. And he will use you cruelly never again.'

To the house of the sorceress there came one night another woman, trembling in the lamplight while the Book of Shadows was flicked from page to page. The visitor was tormented by a hag of the village who kept her from her sleep.

'Each night there is a wailing in the chimney and a pounding on the door,' said she. 'And when I peep from behind the curtains I see her standing there, crooked as a bough, with a shawl wrapped about her shoulders. I'm thinking she's a spawn of the Devil, for she never lies in her bed at night.'

Before the clock struck once more the tormented one was away, with a strange task to perform.

In the churchyard she was to scratch earth from a Christian woman's grave, and lie with it sprinkled under her pillow. And to keep Satan at bay she was to recite the word *agia* over and over in her prayers. This enchanted word, the sorceress explained, formed the initial letters of the ancient Hebrew *Athah gabor ieolam, Adonai* (Thou art powerful and eternal, Lord).

To repel the hag of the village she was to burn a candle in a secluded nook, and watch while the flame shed its light. While it glowed, her tormentor would be stricken with a raging fever; and when it expired so would the hag's life span.

'As the flame flickers and burns low,' the woman was told, 'there will be no more wailing in the chimney. Instead you will hear the croaking of a raven there – a sure omen that the messenger of death is near.'

For a handsome reward Anne Bodenham once shared a treasured secret with an adventurous scholar of Andover – an earnest young man with a strange longing.

He had studied the movement of heavenly bodies and had spent much time pondering the mysteries of Stonehenge.

'If only I could journey beyond the clouds,' said he wistfully, 'and fly among the stars as witches and goblins are said to do. What wonders I would discover!'

The sorceress looked at him suspiciously. 'Truly a bold venture for mortals,' she murmured. 'Not even an eagle can soar so high.'

But she saw the sparkle in his eyes; and gold coins glistening in the lamplight. And she drew her chair a little closer. A sorceress less skilled than she would have hung her head and sent the young man away. It was a challenge that her mentor, the far-famed Dr Lam might have declined. But she was undaunted.

Many days of searching and long incantations lay ahead: spells to recite, rare herbs to gather, and potions to brew. 'Come again when the moon is new,' she said.

In the pages of her book the formula was found, written in ink that had faded with age. She held the lamp close to decipher the recipes recorded there for witch's ointment and the special draught one must sip to soar high above the church steeple. One by one and over and over she spelled out the directions until she had learned them by heart.

Beware, ye who pick of the monkshood, for one pinch leads to passion, two to death. Little friar, whose blue bells tinkle at the garden's edge, what venom flows through they veins?

Powdered bones of the hangman's prey, ground in the blood of a bat.

Crushed parsley, mint and the leaves of poplar, steeped in lard and sprinkled with the flower of sweetflag.

Sweet purple of the belladonna, who plays the Devil's part, mixed with soot and the juice of cowbane.

When the new moon showed in the sky, the young man of Andover came knocking once more on the sorceress's door. With a smile she led him in.

For seven nights now the witch's ointment had fermented in a jar, its lid tightly fastened so that no whiff of its magic should escape. The young man took it eagerly, his heart beating fast.

On the first day of August, the summer festival of Lammas, he was to go at nightfall to a secluded spot on the plain, and there annoint his body from head to foot, while he squatted astride a bough of hawthorn.

The young man listened attentively. Then into his hand she pressed a phial – the potion he was to taste. She clutched at his sleeve. 'But, beware!' she warned. 'Don't fly too high. One drop from the phial will take you to the stars. One more and you will never return!'

When the first night of August came, the young man of Andover went alone to a knoll on Salisbury Plain. There he stood, sky-clad, smearing the witch's ointment all over. Then, mindful of the sorceress's warning, he placed on his tongue one drop of the potion she had given him.

For a while the moon and stars revolved before his eyes – slowly at first, and then with a velocity that made his head spin. With visions of the ground rushing by, he stretched out his arms like the wings of an eagle, and held the hawthorn bough between his knees.

'Faster! Faster!' he cried, raising his head to look up into the heavens. But the moon grew no bigger, nor the stars brighter.

In an urgent desire to soar among them, he waved his arms frantically. Then, in desperation, he put the phial to his lips once more and drained the mystic potion to the last drop. Almost immediately he was overwhelmed with a sensation of falling faster and farther into a fathomless pool of darkness.

The adventurer of Andover was never to remember that a little of the juice of the monkshood, the hemlock and the deadly nightshade invoked hallucination and fantasies, and that just a little more brought death.

It is recorded that for many years Anne Bodenham practised the art of alchemy and divination, until she was betrayed by a servant girl, Ann Styles.

In her deposition the girl exposed her mistress's dark deeds. She told how sometimes she threw a cloak over her body and changed into a black cat; how once she had been persuaded to sign her name in the Devil's book.

Following her trial at Salisbury in 1653, Anne Bodenham was convicted as a witch and sent to the gallows. It is believed that the Book of Shadows was burnt.

And so it was that her treasured secrets, and those of her former master, went with her to the grave.

The Gipsy's Curse

The Brecon Beacons, a range of hills in the heart of South Wales, derive the name from their use long ago as sites for signal fires. If at that time you had travelled from Taf Fechan to Llanfrynach, from Fan Fawr to Talybont, your paths would have wandered over hills, along valleys, and around deep, silent lakes.

And had you strayed beneath the shoulder of Twyn-du, you would have come upon a farmhouse of shaly stone, hidden in the shadows. There lived Old Trickett, a shepherd with leathery skin and a heart of stone, although he was known to have braved a winter blizzard to rescue his sheep from snowdrifts among the crags.

One evening a gipsy woman passed that way. On her arm hung a basket of heather gathered from the hillside, and her pockets were heavy with charm stones picked from the mountain streams. These trifles she would peddle in the villages to the north, for food or an old blanket to keep her warm at night. Close beside her was a scrawny boy dressed in rags. Boldly she knocked on the shepherd's door, and Old Trickett appeared, staring at his unexpected visitor.

'A spray of heather to brighten the windowsill?' the gipsy muttered. 'Charm stones to bring fair weather and good fortune?'

The old man scowled. 'I want no weeds or charms from a beggar-woman!' was his surly reply.

'Then just a copper to buy a loaf of bread for the young one.' She raised the boy's shirt to show his bony frame. 'He's had nothing but berries and turnips from the fields for two days or more.'

Old Trickett brandished his stick; and when the woman was reluctant to leave the threshold he struck out angrily, raining blows upon her arms. As his voice was raised and the door opened wider, his dog leapt at the intruders, growling and baring its teeth. The child cried out in fright and clung to his mother's skirt.

They backed away, the woman kicking at the snarling animal and drawing the boy close to her side. Their clothes were torn, and blood trickled from the child's leg before Old Trickett fastened a leash around the dog's neck and held it back. The gipsy woman turned to stare, hate burning in her eyes.

Wearily they made their way over the hills, the boy limping behind his mother as visions of revenge smouldered in her thoughts.

As night fell they found a shallow cave. There she bathed her young son's wound and laid him to sleep. Then, leaving him curled by the fire, she wandered off in search of bits and pieces with which to fashion an image of the old man with no pity or compassion.

All night she searched and wandered, muttering curses to herself. From cliff top to the valley brooks she scrambled; from the mountain side to a far off churchyard.

For its skin her witch-doll had the scorched fur of rats. The limbs of a toad were stitched on for hands and feet. Into this skin rare herbs were stuffed, first crushed and simmered in the flames. For bones she chipped white quartz from a high crag, and for sinews and muscles she gathered weeds from a neglected garden and rushes from a stagnant pool. Pine gum and water worms were added to the recipe, and last the heart of a black cockerel.

Her devilish brew was mixed with clay from a river bed on which moonlight shone, then moulded into a witch-puppet. Every feature was fixed upon the face – ears, nose, lips with a surly grimace, and for its eyes berries from the ivy in the church-yard.

When her grisly task was done she breathed into the puppet's mouth, as though to bring it life. Then, reciting a sinister spell, she drew it through the ripples of a mountain stream and dried it, first in the night air and then over the flames of her fire.

There was a glint in the gipsy woman's eyes, and the screech of her laughter echoed through the valley below when she clutched a splinter from a broken looking-glass and thrust it into the doll's chest.

It is believed that during the night, far away in his home of shaly stone, Old Trickett cried out in his sleep with a searing pain in his heart. It was a long time before he was found there, lying so cold and still.

The Old Hag of the Mountains

At the turn of the century there was an old woman who drifted from place to place around the Vale of Ewyas and the hamlets in the shadows of the Black Mountains in South Wales. No one knew her name or where she came from, so she was known as the Old Hag of the Mountains, for when she was weary she laid her head to rest in a cave among the mountains.

She fed herself mainly on potatoes and turnips which she stole from the farmers' fields. Occasionally the fleece and bones of sheep she had slaughtered and the ashes of a log fire were found in the caves. Come summer or winter she always looked the same, with long, dark clothes and a black shawl over her shoulders. And through the woods and meadows she roamed, calling at farmhouses and cottages, peddling charms and garlands of wild flowers, and telling the fortunes of those who would spare her a copper.

Many a strange tale is told of the Old Hag of the Mountains. The following accounts of her witchcraft were gathered by children from that quiet county of Brecknock (now renamed Powys), who persuaded their great-grandparents to search through their memories to recall tales remembered by their forbears.

Late one summer evening, two farmworkers near the village of Pandy were leaving the fields after their day's work when they saw the figure of a woman dressed in black standing all alone on the heath. Her shoulders were bent and her head was turned to one side looking up at the clouds. They heard her croaky voice reciting a spell; and when she raised her arms the sky went dark and the sea of golden corn in the field tossed and swayed in a sudden wind. Before long a fierce storm came over the Black Mountains.

All through that night lightning lit up the hills and valleys and thundery rain swelled the streams. Before morning the heath and farmlands south of Wiral Woods lay under flood. The farmer was distressed to see his crops ruined. But as she looked down from her cave in the hillside the old hag chuckled to herself, for she well remembered how all summer long he had set his dogs on her whenever she was found trespassing in his fields.

It was late in the afternoon and dusk had fallen when the rector came upon the Old Hag of the Mountains just beyond Llanthony Church.* She was wandering alone outside the churchyard. Then she entered through the gate and passed the cleric on the path leading from the church. He smiled and bade her good evening, but she shuffled by without a word. To the farthest corner she went, stumbling over the burial mounds and treading on the flowers.

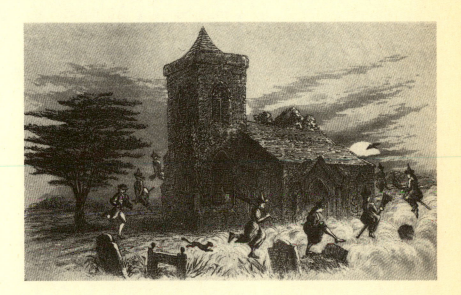

**'. . . he was astonished to see misty shapes
emerge from the shadows among the graves.'**

* Llanthony Church takes its name from the Welsh *Llanddewi Nant Honddu* (St David's church by the Honddu stream). St David, patron saint of Wales, is thought to have spent part of his life there in the sixth century. The church, which dates from the twelfth century, may occupy the site of his monastic cell. It was so aligned that the altar faced directly toward the rising sun on 1st March – St David's Day. During the Middle Ages the building served as a hospital for the priory and the surrounding district.

He stood and watched her until her crooked form was lost in the darkness. Then he was astonished to see misty shapes emerge from the shadows among the graves. The ghostly coven formed a circle, and in the failing light he fancied he saw the old hag at its centre. There was a muttering of voices as they gathered together, and the silhouettes of trees and a harvest moon showed right through them.

The rector murmured a prayer and hurried from the churchyard. When he arrived home he burned a candle in the window and tied a piece of red ribbon to his daughter's crib to protect the child from evil spirits.

One day some children from the village of Llanthony were playing together in Wiral Woods which lies at the foot of the Black Mountains. Shafts of sunlight came slanting down through the foliage. They had not noticed how quiet the woods had become for a summer's day – no birds were singing, no woodpeckers tapping in the boughs.

Presently an old woman came along the woodland path. She walked with a stoop, and a black shawl was draped over her shoulders. They stopped playing and hid among the trees as she approached.

'It's the Old Woman of the Mountains!' a girl whispered, recognizing her hunched shape and long, dark clothing.

'Hag!' shouted one of the boys.

'Old Witch!' called another.

The old woman peered into the woods. Her face was withered. Her eyes burned. The children continued to taunt her from the safety of their hiding place; but when she shuffled closer they ran off, out of the shadow of the woods and across the meadow towards the ruins of Landor House.

They looked over their shoulders as they entered the copse surrounding the ruin, but the old woman was nowhere in sight. The only living creature they saw was a crow, flying low over the meadow behind them. Farther and faster it flew, and then perched on a wall of the ruined house. Its sharp eyes and hooked beak and angry squawk were so like the features of the old woman that they ran off again in fright.

Through wood and meadow they fled, with the crow swooping

and soaring about them, until they came in sight of the priory walls. There the bird gave up its pursuit and circled overhead for a while. The next moment it was gone.*

Beneath the remaining arches of the priory they stood, breathless and afraid. As they looked back towards the copse they saw that the crow had gone from the sky, and the figure of an old woman with a black shawl wrapped about her was moving away across the meadow in the direction of the Black Mountains.

Sometimes in winter, when snowdrifts lay on the hills, a shepherd led his sheep to pasture in the Vale of Ewyas. One day a withered old woman crossed his path. His collie snapped at her heels and, with an oath, the shepherd drove her off because he well remembered how sheep had strayed from the flock or disappeared from the fold, never to be seen again. The old woman stared at the shepherd as he plodded on down into the valley, guiding his sheep along with the aid of his dog and his crook.

From that day on, whenever he descended the mountain path on his way to pasture, his sheep were tormented by a large crow which screeched and squawked among the flock, sending them scurrying in all directions. He would wave his crook and call and whistle while the collie rushed around in confusion.

This wild chase would continue down the mountain side and across the meadow until the sheep had scampered over a stream to the north of Wiral Woods. There the crow would fly away to the west and disappear among the trees.

---

* It has always been believed that witches and evil spirits are loath to enter holy places and that they do not have the power to follow anyone farther than the middle of the next running stream.

143

Old Moll

Aud Mally, who roamed the villages of Teeside in the north-east of England, had a namesake who is remembered in the Gower Peninsula on the southern coast of Wales – a land abounding in tales of witches and the Fair Folk.

No one knows for sure where she lived, and the time when she is said to have wandered her favourite haunts varies from the middle of the seventeenth century to the early reign of George III in the mid-eighteenth century. If the chronicles are to be believed, Old Moll's life spanned a hundred years.

They say she combed the beaches at Brandy Cove, and slept at night in the caves beneath the downs. In the villages of Pennard and Bishopston she was often seen shuffling from door to door, where dogs barked and suspicious eyes peeped from behind the curtains. But wherever she was found, Old Moll was always alone, for she had no friends or relatives.

Many were the stories of her wiles and spells. A villager who drove her off found his house infested with rats. The young son of another met demons in his sleep. Whenever she was cruelly treated, misfortune struck the culprits. Cattle ailed, crops withered, children were plagued with nightmares . . .

'The old hag is a witch!' villagers declared. and they set their dogs free to torment her, or hurled stones in her path until she slunk off to the quiet of the common, muttering curses over her shoulder.

Once the children from the village of Pennard were stricken with a mysterious sickness, from which they coughed and choked and fought for breath.

'It's Old Moll who has brought this curse upon us!' their parents swore. And they all agreed that they would not be free of her mischief until the witch was dead and gone. 'Throw her over the cliffs, and let the gulls feed on her carcass!' cried one mother bitterly.

But try as they may, they could not lay hands on Old Moll, for although she was old and unsteady on her feet, she would wrap her shawl about her head, and by some spell change herself into a hare. Then, with newfound speed and cunning, she would elude her pursuers.

Those were the days when it was believed that a silver charm would dispel unwelcome spirits and the curses brought about by witchcraft. So the villagers searched their homes for buttons and coins of silver. From these the blacksmith forged shot for their guns.

Day after day they waited for Old Moll to come along. But it was not until one summer evening that her hunched form appeared on the edge of the wood beyond the churchyard. She was picking her way among the trees, gathering kindling for her fire.

When she caught sight of the angry villagers drawing near, Old Moll crouched low and wrapped her shawl about her. It was not the figure of an old woman they saw retreating to the shelter of the woods, but a furry shape darting through the undergrowth. So swiftly did the creature move that it was visible only for fleeting moments.

Amid cries of anger and bursts of fire, startled birds took to the sky, and the hare fled in terror. It was more by chance than marksmanship that during the chase a stray pellet found its mark. There was a pitiful animal whimpering as the quarry lay writhing under the bracken, its leg hanging limp and bleeding.

Bloodstains were found where Old Moll was last seen. But although the search continued until nightfall, the wounded creature was never captured.

It was dark when Old Moll ventured from her hiding place and stole away.

Never again was she seen combing the beaches at Brandy Cove, nor roaming village streets. But that was not the end of Old Moll. From time to time she appeared farther to the north, wandering the hills and cwms of Glamorgan. And wherever she went, she walked with a limp and carried a stick to help her along.

Corpse Candles

Long ago there was a belief among the folk of Wales that a shining omen – a spectral candle – foretold death or tragedy. The *Canwyll Corph*, as it was known, was said to appear along funeral paths or over the place of impending disaster. It is written that St David himself had asked in prayer that his people be given this sign, the better to prepare themselves for death, and to strengthen their faith in the hereafter.

At that time many educated men believed in such visions, which today would be described as hallucinations. A scientific explanation suggests that marsh gas is sometimes ignited and sets dry vegetation ablaze. Such phosphorescent light, hovering over marshy ground, is popularly known as Will-o'-the-wisp or Jack-o-lantern.

Whether natural or imaginary, at a time when superstition reigned, a phantom glow in the dark struck fear into the hearts of those to whom it appeared.

It was such a vision that came to William Griffith, a seaman of Llanasa in the old county of Flintshire, and led to the examination of Dorothy Griffith, a spinster of the parish, accused of practising witchcraft. An account of the incident is recorded in Flintshire's Historical Society Publications.

Llanasa was a small seaside village of little more than two hundred households. Evidence of the village's close-knit community is illustrated in the local parish register which records that of 238 marriages performed during the quarter century 1672–1697, only twenty-five of those involved came from outside the parish. At that time a large proportion of the inhabitants were seafarers.

Our story begins one winter evening in the year 1655. In their testimony, Thomas Rogers, an alehouse keeper, and his wife

Margaret, described how William Griffith entered the tavern 'about eight of the clock, looking something wild and much affrighted'. In this troubled state he crossed the threshold and made his way towards the cellar where no light burned, stumbling down the steps in his haste and fear.

Anxious for the safety of their visitor, and concerned at the frenzied look about him, the tavern keeper's wife lit a candle and followed him down the steps. She found him cowering in a corner among the dust and cobwebs. When the candle-light shone on him he covered his eyes, uttered a strange cry and fell into a swoon.

The woman called for help, and Griffith's two brothers, who were drinking in the room above, ran to her aid. Because she was pregnant, the tavern keeper's wife was afraid to go near the huddled form, and even less inclined to attempt to raise it from the floor.

Between them the brothers carried William upstairs and laid him on a settle beside the fire. Eventually he opened his eyes, but cried aloud again, and tried to shield the light of the flames from shining on his face.

He lay there for more than two hours, falling into one faint after another. Whenever his senses returned for a moment he pressed his hands against his eyes, as though each flicker of light filled him with terror. In his delirium he was several times heard to mutter the name of the spinster, Dorothy.

After a time they put him to bed in a darkened room, and kept watch over him through the night, hoping that his fever and fright would go away. Once when he woke he pleaded that he should remain hidden there. 'If you turn me out,' he whimpered, 'I shall never be found again!'

An explanation of William Griffith's extraordinary behaviour is revealed in an extract from his own testimony, given under oath to the Justice of the Peace for the county of Flintshire.

That evening, he explained, he was passing along the marshland near the church, continuing on his way to his ship which lay anchored at the Point of Ayr. Outside the graveyard there appeared a host of lights like the flickering of candle flames or the glow of lanterns.

'To the best of my imagining,' he continued, 'the figure of the woman Dorothy Griffith was lingering there among the lights. For about half of a quarter of an hour she moved along beside me, like a ghost rose from the tomb, not speaking a word as she stared at me!'

He recalled that after a while the woman vanished from his sight. But the cluster of lights remained, hovering above the ground and burning as brightly as beacons, showing his way through the darkness.

On and on he followed, held spellbound in their glow, not knowing what lay in wait at the end of his journey.

He thought that perhaps when he came to the tavern of Thomas Rogers the sound of voices from within broke the spell, for then he was able to tear himself free of the *Canwyll Corph* and seek refuge inside.

'So bewitched was I,' his testimony continued, 'that there is no memory of what happened after that – what I done or what was done unto me all that night long till the dawning of the next day . . .'

In his deposition, Edward Griffith, older brother of William, added another chapter to the story, which told of the bitterness between his brother and the spinster Dorothy. Although the accused and her accuser shared the same surname, there was no blood relationship. There was only a long-standing hatred that had smouldered over the years.

Earlier that evening, Edward had met his brother when he was on his way to Point of Ayr. Together they had visited another tavern near the marsh, where they had stayed until after dark. Edward remembered how uneasy his brother was when he saw the spinster Dorothy passing by the window.

'She stopped for a spell and stared at him from outside,' he explained. 'And William was wondering fearfully why she followed him for he had done her no harm . . . The more he drank the more he shook with fright . . . And when I looked again she was gone . . .'

Presently he had left the tavern to meet another brother at Thomas Roger's alehouse. William could not be persuaded to accompany him 'for fear of the woman waiting for him in the dark'.

It was morning when William Griffith showed signs of recovering from his fainting fits. Even in the daylight when his father had arrived to take him home on horseback, he was afraid to venture outside until he knew the whereabouts of the woman who tormented him. So his father and brothers went to the house of the spinster Dorothy and persuaded her to come to his bedside.

According to further testimony from Edward, confirmed by the alehouse keeper's wife, '. . . and she came into the room, saying good words tending to prayer, and protested that she had not come upon William out of doors for a fortnight since . . .'

The spinster's prayer for William's recovery drove much of his fear away. He reached out his hand to touch her; and when he was sure she was not a ghost, he consented to go home with his father.

However, William Griffith continued to harbour a grievance against the woman, even while she was confined in prison on suspicion of a felony.

She petitioned the Lord Chief Justice of Flint, drawing attention to their long-standing emnity and the false accusation that had been brought against her.

An unusual feature of the trial was the number of parishioners who supported her. A petition signed by prominent members of the community stressed the quarrels that had persisted over the years between her and her accuser, and testified that there were no grounds for supposing the spinster to be a witch. Witnesses for her defence included members of the church, a baronet and a royalist captain in the civil war. At a time when so many fell victim to persecution, the accused was fortunate to have influential neighbours to vouch for her good name.

When Dorothy Griffith appeared before the Assizes more than three centuries ago she was aware that hearsay evidence often secured the conviction of witches. The judges who were appointed to examine her had only recently sentenced to hanging three Cheshire women, after taking into account the unsupported evidence of children.

There were two factors which weighed heavily in her favour and influenced the judges' verdict. The evidence of her accuser, who had spent most of the evening drinking at an alehouse was hardly reliable. And no one, other than he, had witnessed candlelights glowing in the dark. But more likely it was the petition endorsed by the fair-minded citizens of Llanasa that saved the spinster Dorothy from the hangman.

Old Hannah

One summer evening a farmer and his young daughter were travelling home from the fair at Haverfordwest, a town in the south-west corner of Wales. The cart trundled along toward the sunset, its wheels rattling on the bumpy road. Lying snug, with her head resting on a bundle of hay, the girl closed her eyes, lulled to sleep by the motion of the cart.

They were approaching Walton West when an old woman appeared at the roadside. Her hair was scraggy grey, held close to her ears by a headscarf knotted under her chin. She wore laced-up boots under her skirts and strode along with her head held high.

The horse shied as she stepped in its path and the farmer pulled on the reins.

'Could I trouble you to give a tired old woman a ride home?' she croaked.

The farmer nodded. Then the old woman hitched up her skirts and hauled herself on to the back of the cart, where she sat down beside the sleeping girl.

They jogged along for another mile or more before the girl opened her eyes and saw the stranger sitting there. She watched the woman's small, bright eyes, and her leathery hands clasped together as she muttered to herself.

'Are you Old Hannah, the w——?' the girl began in a whisper, and then hesitated as the bright eyes met hers. Tales of the Witch of Walton West were well-known, and it was never wise to rouse her anger. She huddled closer into the bundle of hay.

'Don't be afraid,' the old woman said. 'Hannah would never harm an innocent child. I had a young one of my own once, God rest her soul.'

'Do you cast magic spells?' the girl ventured, a spark of interest in her eyes.

Hannah chuckled. 'Never wicked spells,' she answered. 'But if the moon shone brighter I could read your fortune in your palm. I could tell your life's span and see the years of happiness that stretch before you, and all the hearts you'll break.'

From the back of the cart they could peep over the hedges where, in the last of the daylight, three teams were harrowing in a field.

'You couldn't stop those teams with a magic spell?' the girl challenged mischievously. 'Only a sorcerer or a queen of the Fair Folk could draw them from their task!'

Hannah chuckled again. 'Watch, young lady,' said she, holding up her arms and stretching her fingers wide as she whispered a spell.

And in a moment the horses of the first team reared in the shafts as though a wall of flame had flared up before them. The second team also reared suddenly, and the farm boy who was holding the reins fled, stumbling over the furrows. But the third team went harrowing along, unaffected by Hannah's spell.

The girl watched expectantly, but still the horses plodded on. 'Perhaps the magic has worn away,' she sighed, shrugging her shoulders in disappointment. 'Only a queen of the Fair Folk casts spells that will last for ever.'

'No spell could ever stop the third team,' Old Hannah explained, 'for the driver has a piece of mountain ash fast to his whip. No witch or demon or lightning storm could bend the furrow he marks.'

'So you're awake at last, my love,' the farmer called, looking back over his shoulder. Then he flicked the horse's flank, and the cart went rattling on towards Walton West.

Bewitched

Sally-Anne lived with her grandmother at Trefelyn, a hamlet close to the shores of Cardigan Bay in West Wales. No one came to visit them at their cottage in the valley because most of the neighbours were afraid of the woman's surly temper. Sometimes it was whispered that she might be a witch. As for Sally-Anne, she was a quiet girl, almost sixteen years old, with dark hair and sad, brown eyes.

Every morning she walked across the hills to Mathry where she worked on a farm just outside the village. There she helped with the housework and tended the animals. She fed the chickens, milked the cows and led them to pasture, and in springtime when the sheep were brought down from the hills she would wander off to watch the lambs frisking in the lowland meadows. She was never more contented than when she was alone with the animals, for she loved them all. Some days she would stay in the meadows for hour after hour while the farmer's wife searched for her everywhere.

'Sally-Anne!' she would call impatiently through the stalls of the byre and around the barn. 'Where on earth can the girl be?'

But Sally-Anne was never to be found. She was always away on the hills or in the meadows. She would pluck sweet apples from the orchard and feed them to the foals. Lambs would run to her side when she called, their tails all atremble. Even the bulls would continue to graze when she came near.

But day after day the washing and the cleaning and all her household chores were left undone while she strayed far from the farmhouse. There were many occasions when the farmer and his wife were obliged to talk to her sternly and remind her of her duties. Then she would frown and explain how the animals would fret if she were not there to care for them. She took little notice of their warning, so one day late on in the spring the farmer called her to the house and sent her home to her grandmother.

'And don't ever come back again!' he told her angrily as the tears welled up in her eyes.

Fearful and disheartened, Sally-Anne made her way over the hills to Trefelyn. When she told her grandmother what had happened the old woman threw up her arms in despair, for the butter and eggs and small wages which the girl brought home was all they had to live on.

That night, while Sally-Anne cried herself to sleep, her grandmother sat before the fire in her rocking chair stroking her sleek black cat. Until long after dark she sat there in the firelight, muttering to herself and stirring the logs until the flames licked high into the chimney.

The following morning when the farmer went to the byre he found his prize bull kicking and snorting, its hoofs tearing the earth floor of the stall. The cows, too, were ill-tempered, lowing and tugging at their chains. With feathers ruffled, the cocks fought in the coop and the hens had not laid. In the meadows the sheep were restive and many of the lambs had followed the ewes into the hills. The plough horse sank to its knees, and no whipping would bring the animal to its feet.

The farmer was puzzled and distressed to see his animals behaving so strangely, for nothing so unusual had ever happened before. And when, throughout the next day, whatever he tried would not console them, he became alarmed.

'It's as though some unknown spell has come over them!' he said to his wife.

That evening, in their cottage across the hills, Sally-Anne and her grandmother sat together in the lamplight. The old woman was rocking in her chair, chuckling to herself. 'Don't fret, child,' she said. 'I'm thinking that before the sun goes down again we'll hear a knocking at the door. That farmer will be sorry he treated you so cruelly, and soon you will be back with your animals on the farm.'

Witches of Llanddona

It was some time in the distant past when an open boat drifted across the Irish Sea and came to rest at an inlet near Llanddona on the east coast of Anglesey. Quite by chance it ran aground there, for there were neither sails nor oars to steer the vessel. Providence alone had carried it safely ashore.

It is more than likely that the wretched voyagers were meant to perish at sea. A cargo of men, women and children – a plague to the villagers on the coast of Ireland – had been cast afloat, exiled from their native land, and left to the mercy of winds and tides.

Dressed in rags, they lay huddled against the timbers, fewer now than when their voyage began. Many had died of thirst and

A witch brewing up a storm from *Historia de Gentibus Septentrionalibus*, by Olaus Magnus, Rome, 1555.

starvation, and their bodies had been thrown overboard. Those who survived looked to the cliffs, wild-eyed, with barely the strength to scramble ashore.

Parched and weak with hunger, they struggled to the beach and sought shelter in the caves. At first the villagers of Llanddona pelted them with stones in an attempt to drive them away. Then they noticed how pitifully helpless were the young ones, and compassion overcame their suspicion of strangers. The exiles were given food and water and cast-off clothing. But they showed no gratitude or friendship in return.

And so it came about that the Witches of Llanddona, as they are remembered, first set foot on the island of Anglesey. The men soon took to thieving and smuggling, while the women, easily distinguished by their long, dishevelled hair and bared breasts, preyed on the local inhabitants, spreading fear among them with their witchery and sinister spells.

The following tales were gathered from the hamlets around Red Wharf Bay, to the north of the Menai Strait.

The Gravedigger

There was once a gravedigger of Llansadwrn who looked up from his toil one day and caught sight of a woman moving furtively among the tombstones. Where flowers lay on the graves she snatched them up and put them in her basket. With her wild hair and ragged clothes she looked like a wandering gipsy. It was fair to imagine that before the day was out she would be calling from door to door, selling violets and daffodils to the villagers.

With a shout, the gravedigger waved his shovel to drive her off. But the woman stared back, muttered an oath, and went about her thieving. Even when he drew close she stood her ground, her bright eyes fixed on him.

'There's no one can see the coloured blooms or breathe in the scent, now that they're dead and gone,' she said bitterly. 'And I have little ones with not a crust to eat.'

The gravedigger had no sympathy for her troubles. He had no children of his own, and his heart was as cold as a tombstone. He seized her basket and flung the flowers back on the graves where they had lain. Then he dragged her along to the churchyard gate and sent her on her way.

From a safe distance she stared back over her shoulder. Her eyes flashed and her lips twisted with hate. 'Go, dig a deep resting place for yourself,' she called to him. 'You will never see the autumn moon. Before the summer flowers have withered, a mound of earth will smother your coffin!'

The days passed, and many times he saw the gipsy outside the cemetery wall. But she never ventured beyond the gate. 'Grave-digger,' he sometimes heard her call, 'there's not much time to dig your own. The summer's wearing on!'

One morning, as he was hard at his task in the corner of the cemetery, he paused to stretch his aching back and to rest in the shade of a yew tree. It was there that he noticed a roughly made pouch of cloth hanging on a branch. It was suspended by a length of cord which drew the neck tight shut.

When it was unfastened he found the most odd assortment hidden inside. There were coffin nails and marble chips and a few coins blackened with age. These lay among locks of hair and musky scented herbs. The gravedigger was not to know that he had come upon a witch's charm bag, left there to hold him in some fearful spell.

That night the crickets chirped around his hearth, and a cock crowed in the dark – a sure presage that the angel of death was calling.

And the angel did not call in vain. The gravedigger was suddenly taken ill. Before the summer had gone he lay buried in the churchyard. There was no stone to mark his grave, and never flowers to remember his passing.

The Talisman

One day a merchant on his way from Pentraeth to the market at Llangoed was obliged to break his journey at Llanddona. His mare was lame and was limping along while he walked at its side, leading the animal on a short rein.

He was relieved to find a blacksmith a short distance along the road. 'Could you spare a few minutes to tend to my horse's shoe?' he called, and led his mount into the stable.

The smithy touched his cap courteously, took his irons from the forge and followed the traveller in. He held the horse's foreleg between his knees and found a sharp nail buried in the hoof. 'The roads are rough hereabouts,' he frowned. 'This poor beast is not the first to suffer. Whoa, steady there, girl.'

When the nail was removed the merchant would have continued on his journey had not the smithy warned that the wound was fresh and the horse should be rested a while.

With true hospitality the stranger was invited into the smithy's cottage to share with him some new-baked bread and cheese and a flagon of ale, while the mare munched hay in the stable. And there he met the smithy's shy young daughter. She had black hair and the darkest eyes, and around her neck she wore a string of seashells and beads which glistened silver and blue when the sunlight caught them.

The smithy and his visitor chatted together as they ate and quenched their thirsts with one flagon after another, while the young girl, Anna, sat quietly at the window, once in a while glancing at the stranger with a smile but not saying a word.

'A charming young lady,' the merchant ventured when he caught her eye. 'More lovely even than my own daughter, waiting for me at home.'

Anna lowered her head and blushed.

'And what a striking necklace!' he said admiringly. 'It's like a talisman that witches wore in days gone by – a string of charms to weave magic spells.'

'She wears it night and day,' the smithy smiled. He replenished his visitor's mug with ale. 'Long ago it was worn by my great-grandmother before she left the old country across the sea. It has been handed down through three generations. Then, when Anna's mother was taken – God rest her soul . . .'

He wiped a tear from his eye and called Anna to the table, where the necklace of charms sparkled like jewels.

'The beads are deep and blue as the summer sky,' he murmured. 'They guard against the evil eye, my great-grannie used to say; and the seashells drive away sickness. Hear how they whisper – like the voices of spirits from long ago.'

The merchant held a shell to his ear, and Anna blushed again at his nearness. But she was not inclined to take the charms from around her neck.

'In her sixteen years she has never known a day's illness,' the smithy went on, 'and fortune always smiles on her.'

He told how she had remained well when fever spread through the village; how nothing could ever harm her while she was protected by her talisman; and how one dark night, when she had lost her way on the cliff-top paths, the shells had whispered and guided her safely home.

The merchant was attracted by Anna's dark eyes, and enchanted with the necklace she wore. How could his riches compare with life-long health and happiness, he reflected. If only his own daughter were so blessed. He imagined her free from sickness and danger. If only the girl would part with her charms. A golden sovereign he would give, or several more, although the necklace was only shells and beads strung together.

But when, before he left, the coins were laid on the table the smithy shook his head, and Anna backed away, clutching the necklace to her breast.

'With so much money you could buy fine clothes and travel far,' the merchant argued. 'A dowry, perhaps, for a wedding day, or a bracelet studded with real pearls . . .'

One by one, more golden coins were laid before them while, wistfully, the smithy looked about the bare walls and well-worn furniture of his cottage, and then into the reproachful eyes of his daughter. He shrugged his shoulders, not knowing what to do. 'It's only a string of shells and cheap beads,' he sighed. 'But to Anna it's more precious than gold.'

Before the merchant continued his journey a pile of sovereigns lay on the table. Sadly the smithy hung his head, while Anna sat weeping at the fireside.

The merchant wore a grin as he called farewell from the doorway, for now the talisman that banished sickness and harboured good fortune was his, and its charms would protect his daughter for the rest of her life.

When horse and rider disappeared over the horizon Anna went to her room. There, in a chest of treasures left her by her great-great-grannie, she found another necklace of beads and seashells and fastened it around her neck. Then, while the sun was still high in the sky, she filled her apron pocket with rusty nails gathered at her father's forge. And when all was quiet she went outside to scatter them along the rough road, wondering if perhaps some other traveller would pass that way before nightfall.

A Witch at Llangefni

Thursday was market day at Llangefni, when the farmers came down from the hills to sell their sacks of oats and corn or select a sprightly ram or two to service their ewes. From all around they came, their carts laden with harvest and sometimes a cow tethered behind.

One morning a gipsy woman and her daughter came to the market place, dressed in tattered clothes. The woman sat on a wooden fence, dangling her legs in a pig pen where the swine squealed and grunted in the mud. A few shillings she clutched in her hand, for she had her eye on a fat hog which would help feed her children through the winter. Her daughter wandered nearby, glancing slyly at rich farmers and their warmly clad children.

When the hog was offered for sale she bid her paltry sum, staring hard at others gathered around her. No one dared offer more, for they feared her piercing eyes and pinched lips.

She fastened a rope around the hog's neck and was dragging it away when, from among the crowd, she heard her daughter crying out. A surly farmer had clutched her by the hair when he felt her hand stealing into his pocket. Angrily he threw her to the ground and beat her with his stick. The gipsy woman tied the hog to the fence and helped her daughter to her feet. Then she turned to the farmer with hate in her eyes. 'Curse the hand that would strike a helpless child!' she muttered ominously.

The farmer was furious. 'Thieves! Whores!' he snarled, snatching back the wallet the girl had stolen from his pocket. 'Your curses can never harm me!'

To add fire to the gipsy woman's anger, he unhitched the hog's tether and sent it squealing through the market place.

Her winter's meat ran off among the crowd, with no one to help her capture the hog.

Before the winter was over, so the story is told, the farmer's hand became withered and hung lifeless at his side.

The Rooky Wood

On a fine afternoon in summer, a young girl from the village of Llanallgo went walking in the woods. Hazy beams of sunlight came slanting through the treetops, and the only sound was the rustling of fallen leaves under her feet.

Here and there she wandered from the paths to admire the white and pink flowers of the wood anemone and the last of the primroses. Then, above the song of the birds, she heard voices laughing in the distance. In a clearing farther along the path she saw three old women sitting together on a grassy knoll. They were not expecting anyone to pass that way, so the girl's appearance there startled them.

When they came towards her she could feel her heart beating faster and was inclined to run away. Each wore a black gown with long sleeves from which their pointed fingers showed. Their eyes shone bright as buttons and grey hair fell to their shoulders.

'Well now, where are you going, my pretty?' asked the one who led the way. 'What's a young maid doing all alone in the woods?'

The coven gathered around her, their bony fingers stretching out to touch her cheek. 'Come, my pretty. Come and talk with us a spell.' Their fingers ran through her hair. 'Why, it's soft and shining like new-spun gold.'

Frightened, the girl struggled free and fled through the trees. Around the trunks and undergrowth she ran, not knowing which way to flee. The wood was dense and the paths were lost. Whenever she glanced over her shoulder the old women were not far behind. She wondered at the speed and stamina of her pursuers. And all the while her legs grew more weary.

When she came to the edge of the woods and crossed a stone bridge over Afon Llugwy she could run no farther. Exhausted, she lay there trembling with fear, waiting for the old women to overtake her. But strangely, no one approached. Her pursuers had vanished.*

Until darkness fell that night, and throughout the following day, the villagers of Llanallgo searched through the woodland with stout sticks of mountain ash. But they found only flocks of rooks angrily squawking at them from the treetops.

The Devil Sisters

From Amlwch to Pentraeth the *Chwiorydd y Diafol* (Devil Sisters) were known and feared along the east coast of Anglesey. With their shrouds of black trailing to the ground and wicker baskets hooked on their arms, they were often seen shuffling along the hillside paths, wending their way from village to village, where they would knock on every door peddling posies of wild flowers or charm stones polished by the mountain streams.

Near Rhoslligwy they called at a farmhouse, beating off a mongrel with their crooked sticks as it growled and snapped at their heels. 'A crust of bread for two hungry travellers,' they begged when the farmer appeared in the doorway.

He looked them over from head to foot, and for a bunch of withered flowers he gave them scraps of meat and a stale loaf of bread, not daring to show his anger when they snatched a chicken from the coop beside the barn, smothering its squawks under the folds of their clothes. He was thankful to see them leave in peace, for the spells of the *Chwiorydd y Diafol* were well known. For his kindness he was spared, but before the day had passed his mongrel's paw was crushed in a rat trap.

At another farm they were refused a handful of turnips and driven from the orchard. And before they were out of sight flames leapt from the stables.

And so it was that wherever they went they left a trail of mischief. At Llanbedre-goch a child who mocked their wrinkled faces was plagued with nightmares; a fisherman who would share none of his catch was drowned in a storm before autumn came. Throughout the parishes those who showed no kindness lost cattle or were stricken with the fever.

At Pentraeth one day they came upon a girl arranging fresh flowers in her basket at the market place.

---

* 'Neither witches nor any evil spirits have power to follow a poor wight any farther than the middle of the next running stream.' *Robert Burns*

'So young and pretty,' she heard one say. 'I wonder what her fortune will tell. Spare a penny for a hungry old soul. Read your palm for a few coppers.'

The girl shook her head. 'A penny will buy a loaf of bread. There are many mouths at home to feed.'

Although she seemed unafraid of the *Chwiorydd y Diafol*, the villagers gathered around were surprised that someone should rouse the witches' anger. 'Give them a copper and be rid of them,' they whispered. 'Who knows what mischief they can weave.'

Again the flower-girl shook her head. 'I've no money to spare for beggars.'

One of the old women stretched out her fingers to touch the flowers. Everyone gasped, expecting the petals to wither or a viper to slither from the basket. But the primroses and violets remained as fresh as the morning dew and nothing stirred from among them. The girl smiled. She had no reason to fear any witch's spell.

The Devil Sisters stared at her, their lips muttering, their eyes burning. 'Perhaps one day you will be hungry, or demons will come to your sleep at night. Beware, my pretty!' they warned.

But the girl turned her back on them, and continued to arrange her flowers. She remembered that five of her sisters were at home, helping on the farm; another lay in Pentraeth churchyard. And it was well-known among country folk that witches hold no power over a seventh daughter.

House in the Shadows

No one knows for sure where the old boarding house was situated. Some say it was beside a wood at Coed-y-Celyn; others believe it stood near Pentre-foelas on the border between Clwyd and Gwynedd. But most agree that somewhere along the fifteen-mile stretch from Cerrig-y-drudion to Betws-y-Coed, at a time when the A5 was a rough road for horse and carriage, there stood a rambling house, hidden in the shadow of trees. Many travellers, on their way from England to Ireland, called there for supper and a night's rest.

Over the years it earned a fearful reputation, and tales of mystery abound concerning the two old ladies who kept the house. So forbidding were the stories that at the time of our account the isolated lodging, Ty-yn-y-Cysgodion (House in the Shadows), was usually deserted. Travellers had told of valuable possessions vanishing during the night, even though their doors and windows were barred. Other rumours told of travellers themselves disappearing, never to be seen again.

One evening a gentleman on his way to Ireland broke his journey at Ty-yn-y-Cysgodion where he decided to rest his horse and proceed in daylight the following morning.

His hosts were two kindly ladies who made him welcome and fed him well. After supper and a mug or two of ale he retired to his room, and when the window and door were securely fastened he curled under the blankets and was soon fast asleep, for his day's journey had been tiring.

He was wakened in the middle of the night by movement at the foot of his bed. The blankets stirred and he heard the sound of soft footfalls running about the room. Startled, he sat up and listened. Then he fumbled to light a candle and searched in the darkened corners. But there was nothing to be seen, and only the sound of the wind sighed in the chimney.

He returned to his bed and slept fitfully until he was wakened again by the sound of someone or something padding around the floor and then leaping up beside him, scratching among the bedclothes. Once more the candle flame showed no intruder in the room; but his clothes were strewn about the floor although the door and window were still fastened.

Looking up, he was astonished to see two pairs of eyes glowing in the darkness above the wardrobe. Then, with a sudden growling and spitting, two cats leapt down at him. He glimpsed their arched backs, bristled fur, bared teeth and claws. He flung one from his shoulder, and grasping a fire iron from the grate, struck out wildly. One of the creatures let out a piercing cry, and together they scampered into the darkness of the fireplace.

The frightened traveller put a match to the kindling in the grate and watched the smoke and flames lick the chimney. But the cats had vanished.

It was a long time before daybreak. He sat in front of the fire, starting at the slightest sound. And there he waited until the first light of dawn showed through the curtains. Only then did he unbolt the door and venture outside.

He discovered that during the night his pockets had been rifled and all his money was gone. But his only wish was to saddle his horse and leave Ty-yn-y-Cysgodion far behind, thankful to escape with his life.

As he hurried through the back door leading to the stable, he heard a voice calling after him, '*A gawsoch chwi noswaith orffwysol?*' (Did you have a restful night?) Looking over his shoulder he caught sight of the other old woman standing in the hallway. At her side one arm hung limply and was swathed in a bandage.

Witchery in Seventeenth-Century Flintshire

. . . a poor beggarly fellow of evil life and conversation, very often drunk and a notorious liar of no credit or estimation amongst his neighbours . . .

. . . a poor woman, worth little or nothing, sharp with her tongue and consorting in the moonlyte with her master the Devil himself . . .

Before 1736, in centuries when the fire of persecution blazed most fiercely, the above descriptions would have been likely to appear on petitions submitted to the Justices of the Peace, bringing to their attention the suspicious characteristics of someone accused of the black arts of sorcery and witchcraft. Yet it was not until the mid-nineteenth century that the superstitious beliefs in such practices died out in Wales.

The following incidents, some recorded in official depositions, others from memories passed from one generation to another, draw a picture of life in the parishes of North Wales long before the sophistication and vagaries of life in the twentieth century.

An Incident at Rhelofnoyd

Recalling memories of a distant generation, which originated with his great-grandfather, an old inhabitant of the county of Flintshire tells of a farmer from the parish of Rhelofnoyd who called one day on his neighbour for payment owed on a sack of corn. This debt the neighbour disputed, and heated words were exchanged. After much argument and hurling of insults the farmer left in a furious temper, with a bleeding nose and an empty pocket.

165

Shortly afterwards, when the neighbour's husbandman was ploughing the fields, his task was interrupted when the oxen fell to their knees, too sick or tired to continue. It was only after much whipping and goading that the beasts made an end of their day's work.

The next morning a similar incident occurred. The oxen were harnessed but refused to drag the plough as they had usually done for many years past. Instead, they staggered along, listless and straying from their path, as though their feed or drinking water had been drugged. Again the husbandman was forced to abandon his task and report the strange sickness to his master.

'The beasts are sick,' he complained, 'or else someone has bewitched them!'

And so the oxen remained out of sorts, eating nothing for more than two days together, lying in their stalls, lowing pitifully, too weak to rise to their feet.

On reflection the master remembered his quarrel with the farmer, who had the reputation of a mean temper and was feared by some for his dabbling in the art of sorcery. So that very evening, after supper and a clumsy prayer of exorcism, he set off across the fields with a pocket jingling with coins to pay for the sack of corn, all the way mumbling a rehearsal of the apology he was to make and a plea to his neighbour to wish the oxen well again.

His money and apology were grudgingly accepted. And, after a dram or two of whisky to bind their reconciliation, they went together to the byre where the oxen were stalled.

In the lamplight the farmer took a pail of water, fresh from the well, and placed three charms into it – a wedding ring of gold and a thimble of silver, both borrowed from the sorcerer's wife, and a heavy black key from the barn, for iron. Next, the spell-binder explained, they should seek a place where the living and the dead pass over. So they trudged along to the churchyard gate where the charms were stirred in the pail of water, and a strange incantation was recited three times over.

When this macabre ceremony had been performed with due reverence they returned to the byre, where the oxen still grunted and lowed. They had refused to drink for a day or more, so now they should be thirsty. When the pail was put before them they lowered their heads, and the silvery water trickled from their muzzles. What remained was poured over their backs and splashed into their eyes.

The following morning, while the cocks were crowing, the oxen were on their feet again, their heads down munching in the trough.

When the husbandman's ploughing was done that day he was sent along to the house of the sorcerer of Rhelofnoyd to offer a few more shillings in payment for the sack of corn. After all, the debt had been long overdue.

The Widow of Penly

'. . . when the sayd Anne is displeased she doth hurte to them and theirs, and further I can not say . . .'

So wrote one deponent of the widow Anne Ellis, who lived in the county of Flintshire during the seventeenth century and was known throughout the parish for her unforgiving ways and skill in the art of witchcraft. She was a beggar who knitted stockings to sell to the villagers and few dared send her from their door, for fear of being stricken with misfortune, brought about by her mischievous spells.

On a winter's morning more than two hundred years ago she was driven from the house of John Byrch of Overton Forren. Before nightfall he was bitterly to regret his action, for without warning his daughter was taken sick, and the symptoms relating to her illness were a mystery to the doctors whom he consulted.

Fearing that the child was bewitched, he went to the house of the widow, Anne Ellis, pleading that she return with him to bless the girl. But she was known always to harbour a grievance, and for four days refused to break the spell, leaving the victim to suffer. It is recorded that:

> . . . the sayd childe fell sike uppon Sunday night, and uppon Munday morneing ther appeared under the left arm a great lump of the bignesse of a hen's egg, the childe continueing in great paine, crying and lying uppon her face trembling . . .

The following deposition gives further evidence of the mischief and vengeful ways of Anne Ellis:

The examination of Elizabeth Jeffreys of Penly, in the county of Flint, taken by Andrew Ellise, esquire, one of the justices of the said county, uppon the theird day of June 1657, conserneing Anne Ellis suspect of witchcraft.

Sworne sayth that about two yeares last past June the daughter of the examinant was very sicke and she feareing because of the reporte that sayd Anne Ellis, of Penley, had done harme to the sonne of Elizabeth Taylor, aforesaid that the sayd Anne might alsoe have done hurte to her daughter, this examinant therefore went to the house of the sayd Anne Ellis and requested her to come see her daughter that lay sicke.

The sayd Anne came and blessed the childe and shortly after the childe recovered, as is knowne to all the neighbours. This examinant sayth that about a month after the recovery of the childe shee was talking with the sayd Anne Ellis conserneing the same. The sayd Anne replied shee could goe to them and put any desease uppon any one.

Not long after, this examinant's sayd childe fell sicke againe in the same manner beeing taken with a swelling all over her body and beeing soe deseased the sayd childe toulde her mother that it was allwayes soe when this examinant fell out with the sayd Anne Ellis and that her sayd daughter dyed of the same distemper aboute Whitsunday the twelvemonth last past.

The examinant further sayth that on Saturday last past Margaret, the daughter of William Hughes, of Penley, came with other children to the house of the sayd Anne and did eate some of her bread in the abscence of the sayd Anne, whereat when shee returned home shee was extreame angry. Whereuppon this examinant desired the sayd Anne not to curse the sayd children nor to do them any hurte, whereat the sayd Anne made noe answere but muttered to her selfe.

This examinant sayth that when the sayd Anne is displeased shee doth hurte, that this examinant uppon Munday morneing the sayd Margaret Hughes was fallen sicke, brought the sayd Anne to the house of the sayd Hughes to see the childe, who was sicke indeed, and the sayd Anne entred the chamber where the childe was sicke in bedd and put her hand on the childe and asked 'How doest thou?' Shee replied 'Very sicke.' Then the sayd Anne, putting her hand uppon the childe sayd 'God blesse thee, thou shalt mend after this.'

And further sayth that shee hath heard an ill report of her the sayd Anne eight yeares and received her into her house more for feare than love, that when shee taxed her for curseing Richard Hughes afforesayd who hath bine a cripple this eight yeares suspected to bee hurte by her, the sayd Anne replied askeing why he did pisse downe her chimney . . .*

According to records, Anne Ellis was committed to the common gaol in the summer of 1657, but cunningly made an escape from the constable. No one knows what became of her. More than likely she spent the rest of her days preying on the superstitions of simple folk.

Witch of Caerwys

Beyond the middle of the eighteenth century it was not possible to seek retribution in the courts for those who practised sorcery and witchcraft. But long after 1736, when justice was tempered with understanding, the inhabitants of rural Wales often took the law into their own hands. Ruthless reprisals such as stoning, lynching and burning were not unknown.

The hamlet of Caerwys stood on the fringe of woodland to the east of the Vale of Clwyd. And there, in a rough log hut long abandoned by the woodmen, lived a gaunt woman who was a fugitive from society. During the daytime she was often seen wandering along hillside paths and village streets. But what she did after dark remained a mystery. Some say she met with the Devil in the churchyard.

Whenever she approached, doors were shut and folk would peep from their windows to watch her go by. 'Raggedy witch! Miserable hag!' bolder children would torment. And when she stopped to stare mothers called the young ones indoors and drove her off with stones.

Bruised and bitter, the poor woman would pull her shawl about her and make her way back to the woodland, with designs of vengeance smouldering in her thoughts. At night she would sit by her fire, nursing her injuries and muttering to the flames.

It was not long before the villagers of Caerwys were troubled by strange happenings in their homes. Cold draughts would set the fires flaring, and smoke would billow from the chimneys. Lamps would flicker and peter out, leaving the children to cry in the dark. Fearful nightmares would wake them from their sleep.

* The examination of Elizabeth Jeffreys by one of the Justices of Flint, concerning Anne Ellis, a suspect witch, is an extract from a study by J. Gwynn Williams, M.A., and appears in the *Flintshire Historical Society Transactions* (1975/6).

'It's the woman from the woods!' an angry mother declared. 'She has put a curse on us!'

Red ribbon was tied over the children's beds. Petals of elder-flower were strewn about the thresholds. But none of their charms could break the spell. At all hours of the night the young ones would scream out in the darkness, telling of ghostly fingers tearing at their tongues, of pillows held fast to their mouths to stifle their cries. As time wore on they were afraid to close their eyes.

Desperate to see an end to their troubles, a band of villagers went to the log hut in the woods. But the woman's door was bolted, and inside she waited silently until they had gone away. Many times they went to find her, for the curse continued unabated and they feared the torment would never end. But each time their journey was in vain. The woman hid in the woods or chuckled at their anxiety from behind her bolted door. Neither their anger nor their pleading could persuade her to withdraw the spell.

It was an old grandmother from the village who set the spark alight. 'Her curse could never reach out beyond the grave,' said she.

So one night a determined band made their last journey to the witch's hut. From the woods they gathered twigs and fallen branches which they heaped at her door. Then they put a torch to it and watched the flames rage. The sky was aglow, and the woods echoed with shrieks of terror.

Hand of Glory

Michael O'Leary was a rogue, like his father before him. As for his grandfather, the renowned Patrick O'Leary, he was perhaps the most cunning thief who ever roamed the villages of County Kildare.

Like Robin Hood of Sherwood Forest and Twm Shôn Catti from the hills and woodland of West Wales, the O'Learys never maliciously harmed a soul, for they always stole from the rich, and shared their ill-gotten gains with those less fortunate.

It was one night, while Michael was rummaging through a chest of his grandfather's keepsakes, that he came upon a cloth-bound book, its pages yellowed with age. Near the back of the book he found a strange verse, written in a language he could not altogether understand.

Could this, by chance, spell out some secret of the old man's cunning, he wondered. He remembered that in all his years of mischief the old man had never been caught. Tales he had heard from his father told of Patrick O'Leary's nocturnal haunts: of how he appeared from nowhere, and then vanished like a spectre in the night.

The writing was faint in the lamplight, so Michael held the book close to the flame, squinting at the words, whispering them to himself one by one. And as he read he grew more excited about his discovery. It told a story of long ago: of Mohareb the enchanter who lulled to sleep Yohak, the giant keeper of the caves of Babylon.

'Lulled to sleep a giant, now did he,' he murmured thoughtfully. 'How b' Jesus would he be doing that?'

He drew the lamp closer still, turning up the wick until the flames danced brightly and wisps of blue smoke curled into the dark.

Michael had little taste for literature, and much of the verse puzzled him. Some lines he read three or four times over, his brow furrowed with concentration. Wrestling with the interpretation was an arduous task, but the thought that he might have stumbled on the old man's guarded secret spurred him on. What if he could solve the mystery of the cloak of darkness no one could unfurl?

Long past midnight he pored over the book, striving to unravel the formula. From beginning to end he spelled out the verse, gleaning scraps of knowledge here and there. Some of the words had completely faded away; others had a meaning he would never untangle.

> Thus he said,
> And from his wallet drew a human hand,
> Shrivelled and dry and black;
> And fitting as he spake
> A taper in its hold . . .

'A human hand stuffed in his wallet, b' Jesus! Now what would he be doing with that? Burnt to a cinder, was it?'

> . . . murderer on the stake had died.
> I drove the vulture from his limbs,
> And lopt the hand that did the deed,
> And drew up the tendon-strings to close its grasp.
> And in the sun and wind
> Parched it, nine weeks exposed . . .

Michael shuddered when he imagined a bird of prey feeding at the gibbet, and the corpse's hand being hacked away.

> Look! It burns clear, but with the air around
> Its dead ingredients mingle deathliness.
> This when the keeper of the caves shall feel
> Maugre the doom of heaven,
> The salutary spell
> Shall lull . . . to sleep
> And leave the passage free.

He could make no sense of the last verse, but continued to turn the leaves of the book, searching among the scribblings until he came upon another rhyme which seemed pertinent to the charm.

Let those who rest, more deeply sleep;
Let those awake, their vigils keep
Oh, Hand of Glory, shed thy light . . .

That night he tossed fitfully in his bed as the words of the poem echoed in his thoughts. '. . . a human hand, shrivelled and dry . . . Draw the tendons to close its grasp . . . And fitting a taper in its hold . . . Lulled to sleep the giant keeper of the caves . . .'

'Then it's a hand of a corpse I'll be needing,' he muttered to himself with a shiver. 'And a candle to burn in its fingers.'

Could this be his forbears' secret – the charm that kept them safe from discovery? More than once he had appeared before the magistrates. But, as far as he could remember, neither his father nor his grandfather, the notorious Patrick O'Leary, had ever been brought to justice. Perhaps this grisly hand with a taper in its grasp would lull to sleep his victims, as it had done to the giant keeper of the caves. Then he could go about his mischief, unhindered.

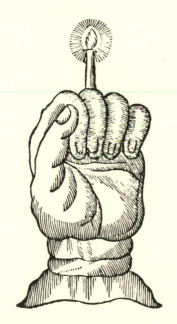

The Hand of Glory.

When at last he fell asleep, Michael dreamed that a cloak of darkness fell upon him, with a torch-bearing hand to show the way. Startled victims stared in wonder, and then surrendered to its spell.

It was a gruesome mission he was undertaking, so he chose a moonless night, when the cemetery was dark and still. Only an owl saw him throw his shovel over the wall and climb into the graveyard. Tombstone shadows danced in the rays of his flashlight. He had already marked the grave to plunder and knew the path to the burial mound.

There were no longer gibbets standing at the cross-roads: no murderers hanging there to feed the vultures. But he had singled out a godless man, interred not long ago.

He dug down deep until the coffin was unearthed. With trembling fingers he unfastened the lid and shone his light upon the mouldering corpse. There was no one to watch the ghoul at work, and only the owl called out.

Before dawn showed, the body was buried again, and the grave snatcher stole away with a withered hand wrapped in a piece of shroud torn from the corpse.

Following the directions written in the verse, he drew the tendons tight, until the fingers curled and seemed to reach up to clutch at his throat. When the strings were fastened he hid it in a stone jar so that the rats could not gnaw at the flesh.

For several weeks it rotted there, until the bones were exposed. Then into its grasp he fixed a torch, made with rope and tallow. He peeped at it from time to time with eager anticipation.

'Beware now, Yohak, sentry of the caves,' he would chuckle mischievously. 'It's a sharp look-out you'll have to be keeping when Mohareb the enchanter comes your way.'

Now that he was to be the Will-o'-the-wisp of Kildare, invisible to all mortals, he chose the grandest house in the county to burgle. There would be precious jewellery and rare ornaments worth a fortune. And besides, the Lord and Lady Hamilton were not Irish born and bred, and showed no charity to the peasants.

It was long after dark when he set out across the fields, wearing a long cloak, black as the night, beneath which he concealed the Hand of Glory.

The house was silent, silhouetted against the sky, and young

O'Leary's heart was beating fast with expectation. Armed with his charm he could wander the corridors of Lord Hamilton's mansion and plunder each room, while the occupants were lulled to sleep.

He hurried through the copse, and was stealing across the lawns when footsteps were heard approaching along the gravel paths. 'Mohareb' had not remembered that the gamekeeper might be on the prowl. But this was of little consequence, he told himself, for wasn't he now shrouded by the enchantment of the Hand of Glory. Moreover, Lord Hamilton's gamekeeper – a mere mortal – could not be compared with the giant keeper of the caves.

'I'll not be fearing the likes of you,' he muttered as the figure drew nearer. So saying, he took the withered hand from beneath his cloak, placed the taper in its fingers and set the torch alight. Boldly he went forward, his charm held high, burning like a beacon and casting pools of green light about his feet. He was curious to see the spell run its course. Would the fellow pass by, unaware of his presence, or would he stare in wonder and then stand petrified with fright?

The gamekeeper was clearly startled, and crossed himself once or twice. But his courage did not falter. First he stared in astonishment. And then, 'Who's there?' he challenged.

O'Leary came on, undaunted. Soon the spell would take effect. Higher still he held the torch, waving it from side to side. 'Hand of Glory, shed they light!' he called aloud as it flared. 'Let those who behold more deeply sleep . . .' At any moment his challenger would be mesmerized by the torch and fall into a trance.

But it so happened that it was O'Leary who fell unconscious, beaten to the ground by the gamekeeper's shillelagh. And when he regained consciousness, his attacker was standing over him.

The commotion was heard indoors, and servants came running from the house. At first, the gamekeeper explained, he thought that the hooded intruder had set himself on fire, for he was crying out crazily, and it seemed that the hand grasping a torch had been burned to the bone.

As for the latter-day Mohareb, he was left to stagger off home, everyone believing that either he was mad or the worse for drink. Although his grandfather's formula had gone awry, he wasn't one to give in easily. In the seclusion of his room he would search again through the chest and study the old man's scribblings. One day he would discover the secret. There was no one more diligent than Michael O'Leary.

POSTSCRIPT

According to the *Dictionnaire Infernal*, by J.A.S. Collin De-Plancy, 1818, the superstition relating to the Hand of Glory was widely held in parts of Spain, Germany and France.

The hand of a gibbeted criminal was cut off and wrapped in a winding sheet, bound tightly to draw out any blood which remained. This grisly souvenir was then embalmed in an earthenware vessel and preserved with a concoction of saltpetre, graveyard weeds, salt and pepper.

After a period of thirteen days it was dried in the sun or baked in an oven until completely parched. A taper, fused with virgin wax or fat rendered from the murderer's flesh, was thrust between the dead fingers.

Until early in the nineteenth century, the Hand of Glory was coveted by thieves, for when the taper was lit, it was believed that anyone approaching the thief about his mischief would be petrified, while he who held the charm would become invisible. Mysteriously, doors that barred his way would open, and the household would remain in a lulled sleep until the flame was extinguished. The spell was supposedly enhanced when the intruder chanted aloud:

> Let those who rest, more deeply sleep;
> Let those awake their vigils keep.
> Oh, Hand of Glory, shed they light
> And guide us to our spoil this night.

One such gruesome relic is presently displayed at Whitby Museum in the North Riding of Yorkshire.

Enter the Devil

This poem recalls a ballad about Cornelius Agrippa, a sixteenth century occultist.

> On the study table a book there lay
>   Which Agrippa himself had been reading that day.
> The letters were written with blood therein,
>   And the leaves were made of dead men's skin.
>
> The young man he began to read
>   He knew not what, but he did proceed,
> When there was heard a sound at the door
>   Which as he read grew more and more.

And more and more the knocking grew;
   The young man knew not what to do.
But trembling with fear he sat within
   Till the door was broke and the Devil came in.

Two hideous horns on his head he had got,
   Like iron heated nine times red-hot.
The breath of his nostrils was brimstone blue,
   And his tail like a fiery serpent grew.

ROBERT SOUTHEY, 1774–1843

Reign of Terror

In 1532 Germany saw the emergence of the Catholic Code – a decree adopted by hundreds of small independent states which at that time comprised the Holy Roman Empire, and which imposed the penalites of torture and death for witchcraft.

During the following century, hundreds of thousands were accused, condemned and burnt for heresy. Throughout the continent of Europe, Germany was more ruthless in its persecution than any other country. An inquisition as merciless as that of the Middle Ages was unleashed to banish the powers of darkness.

Once accused, by gossip or suspicion, the victims were presumed guilty and only a few were able to establish their innocence. The variety of disreputable witnesses, including young children and convicted heretics, were often unknown and unseen by the defendant. The accused was allowed no counsel, for then the lawyer himself would be considered guilty of defending heresy. When charges were denied, torture was inflicted to extract confessions and the names of accomplices, even if others were falsely implicated.

Victims drawn into the clutches of the Inquisition had little chance of escaping a terrible fate. A German scholar, describing the torture chambers, declared that the most courageous who suffered there would confess to any crime and welcome death ten times over rather than endure another hour at the mercy of their tormentors.

One of the most pitiful records in the annals of witchcraft trials relates to Johannes Junius, the Burgomaster of Bamberg early in the seventeenth century. While in gaol awaiting execution he spent his days recording the tragic events of his questioning and torture. The gaoler had been bribed for scraps of paper and a promise that when the prisoner's body had been burned, his last thoughts be given to his sole survivor.

Wo du Gedult hast in der Pein,
So wird sie dir gar nützlich seyn
Darumb gib dich willig darein.

The Bamberg witch trials in the 17th century.

A Thousand Goodnights

Dated 24th July, 1628, the letter began: 'A thousand goodnights, my beloved daughter, Veronica.' The handwriting was barely legible, because the prisoner's fingers had been crushed and distorted by the torturer's thumb-screws.

'Innocent I come into prison, and innocent I must die. For whoever comes into the witch prison must become a witch – or suffer in the hands of the torturer.'

Over many days, each word was painfully recorded. He told of his arrest and of how he had protested his innocence. 'I come here through falsehood and misfortune. I am no witch, and have a pure conscience. Even though they bring witnesses and the executioner, I will swear to it.'

During the time when he was writing this letter to his loved one, Johannes Junius was put to further harrowing torture. Thumb-screws were fastened upon him and both hands bound together, so that blood spurted from beneath his nails. 'You are a knave – a witch!' his examiners would cry. 'Confess it freely. Höppen Ellse has seen you dance at night on Hauptsmorwald.'

'Thereafter they stripped me,' his letter continued, 'binding my hands behind my back and fastening weights about my ankles. Eight times did they draw me up on the ladder until my head reached the pulley itself. For some time I hung there, so that my limbs were stretched by the hanging weights and almost torn from my body. Then, by slackening the rope, I was let down each time with a jerk, until my feet were not quite on the ground. I cannot tell what agony I suffered.'

At the end of his ordeal the Burgomaster was dragged back to his cell, his arms and legs disjointed. There, a more compassionate gaoler begged that he confess. 'Good sir, you can never endure the torture which you will be put to. Own that you are truly a witch, for only then will your suffering be at an end.'

But Johannes Junius remained steadfast in his denial. 'God forgive them for misusing an innocent and honourable man,' he muttered. He pleaded that he be given a day for thought and words with a priest. The priest's attendance was refused, but he was granted a day for reflection.

There followed interminable hours of interrogation and torture. With no window in the underground chambers, day and night was one long stretch of darkness, broken only by the glow of torches burning at the wall. So excruciating was his torment that at last he relented so far as to confess with his lips, yet not with his heart.

'Then, from my imagination, I told of a witch sabbat,' his story went on. 'I had not recognized, nor could I remember those who had gathered there.'

'Was not your friend, the Burgomaster Dietmeyer, at the sabbat?' his examiners insisted. 'Speak, or we shall put the torturer at your throat again!'

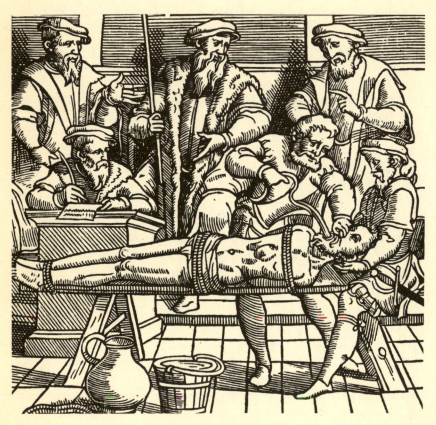

A witch being tortured.

'May God forgive me,' he wrote. 'I nodded my head, for I could endure no longer. "And who besides?" they demanded. And so continuously they urged that I name all whom I could recall – from the market place, then the Zinkenwert, and along the street to the bridge over the Georgther. Many persons did I name, though the poor souls are as innocent as I.

'For fear of scalding baths, leg vices, and burning torches held under my arms, I searched my imagination for further heresy they forced me to confess. Although my heart remains true, my lips told of renouncing God, of stealing wine from the church, and of burying sacred wafers in unhallowed ground on Hauptsmorwald.'

Burgomaster Junius' letter to his daughter ended as sadly as it began. 'Dear child, keep my words secret, and let no one see this message, for if God sends no way of bringing the truth to light, you too may share my fate.

'A thousand goodnights, for your father will never see you again.'

Together with many others, Johannes Junius was tied to a stake and burned in a public square at Bamberg during that summer of 1628.

Witch burning in Germany in the 16th century.

Shinterin the Bone Breaker

A trial at Eichstatt in 1637 brought to light tales of sabbats, sky-clad night riding, and necromancy – the art of communicating with those beyond the grave.

The accused was a deluded old woman who laughed hysterically when she was brought before her examiners. There was no fear in her eyes. 'No harm can befall me,' she chuckled, 'for the Master will watch over his own.'

She told how one day her Master, the Devil, had come to her in the guise of a hangman, with a cloak about his shoulders, a noose held in his hand, and eyes glowing like fire behind the mask he wore. His limbs were furred and his footfalls showed the marks of cloven hoofs. 'No mortal can win back my soul!' the demented woman challenged. 'No grave can hold me quiet!'

There is no record of her given name. She was remembered only as Shinterin the Bone Breaker, because that was the name with which Satan summoned her. It was his bidding that with devilish spells she steal the souls of the righteous. These spells were cast in the moonlight on Walpurgisnacht, before the first cock crowed on the first day of May.

In the churchyard, bones of the long departed were dug up. The grisly burden was bundled into the old woman's apron and carried to the hills. There they were broken up and laid on the ground in a circle measuring some two metres across. A fire was lit inside the circle, and while it burned she stood beside the flames reciting the words of a spell she had learned from the Master.

Satan, the woman declared, favoured her above others. Sometimes he had been her lover, brutal in his fornication, and jealous of mortal men who laid with her. He had taught her to brew a potion which quietened her husband whenever he came to her. And with torment and poisonous herbs they had sent him to an early grave.

'The Master remembers me still,' the old woman said, recalling how, only the night before, he had come to visit her in her cell.

That Shinterin the Bone Breaker was a witch there was no mistaking. Freely she owned to consorting with the powers of darkness and casting spells to torment countless God-fearing men and women. Witch's marks were found on her throat and breasts and shoulders.

Only when she was tortured to the verge of madness did she name many of the villagers as her accomplices. It is said that her confession stirred up a surge of persecution in Eichstatt which led to the conviction and deaths of several hundred supposed heretics, including those of mean and noble birth, the virtuous, the ungodly, and innocent children too young to understand the difference.

Had she been condemned in England, she might well have met her lover, the hangman, at the scaffold. But in Germany witches were burned.

Ironically, she cheated both the hangman and the torch bearer, for the torture and ill-treatment by her gaolers was more than her frailty could endure. She died in prison the night before her pyre was to be lit.

Anna Maria Schwagel

Long after the cruel laws relating to witchcraft had been repealed in other European countries, the practice of sorcery and consorting with dark spirits remained a capital offence in Germany.

One of Europe's last trials for witchcraft took place in Bavaria in 1775. Standing accused was a love-lorn servant girl, Anna Maria Schwagel.

As her story unfolded it was learned how she had fallen under the spell of a coachman who boasted of his skill at black magic and of his association with demons. 'Come with me where the wolf's bane blooms,' he would entice, 'and you will learn secrets hidden from all others – secrets you have never dreamed of!'

Together they would journey in his coach to lonely glades, there to keep company with a coven of witches and devil worshippers who revelled all night long, until the moon went pale and dawn showed through the trees. 'Our naked bodies were smeared with an ointment,' the girl recalled. 'And rare herbs were brewed which stirred us to fornication and wild dancing. In the moonlight we moved like wraiths above the ground, and the Master came among us, embracing all the young girls in turn. His kisses were cold as the mountain snow.'

She further confessed that at the sabbats she mocked her Catholic faith and made a covenant with the Devil.

Through summer and autumn they journeyed together. But as winter drew on, Anna Maria's fortune changed. She discovered that the coachman, her lover, was untrue. He tired of her when he found another, more brazen and fair than she. Forsaken now by her family and shunned by the villagers, she ran away to wander the streets of Kempten, begging for food and shelter, and a willing prey for all lechers.

Witches at a sabbat. Sabbats were secret meetings for practitioners of witchcraft, sorcery or devil worship.

Eventually, destitute and wasting with sickness, she was given refuge in a home for waifs. There she was clothed and fed, and although in time she grew a little stronger, she was forever troubled with fearful dreams, crying out in her sleep as though she were possessed by devils.

Unable to bear her torment any longer, she sought forgiveness for her past misdeeds, telling of ungodly rituals in the quiet glades, of a lover who held her under his spell and led her along the paths of wickedness.

Although repentant of her wrongdoing, and bearing no malice towards her former lover, Anna Maria's confession spelled the end of the coachman. He was apprehended and condemned as the Grand Master of a coven, and was to suffer the extreme penalty. Judged by the magistrates as a willing disciple, the servant girl shared his fate. Both were beheaded, and their bodies were burned in the market square.

By a cruel quirk of fate, had she yielded to temptation only a few years later her punishment would have been reproach for her transgression and a prayer for the salvation of her soul.

The Night Riders

A parish priest, describing the reign of terror which prevailed in Germany, told of chancellors, professors, students and monks who fell victim to the witchcraft hunt. Falsely accused, these and a host of others were persecuted and put to death for heresy.

'Children of three and four years old were said to consort with devils . . . On the eve of our Lady's Day there was executed here a girl of nineteen – the loveliest and most virtuous in all the city who, from her childhood, was raised by the Prince-Bishop himself . . .'

Thereafter, a wave of sympathy for the unfortunate victims spread through the land, until at last the witch hunt had run its course. But when the flames of the pyres had burned out and the ashes had blown away, there emerged a cult as evil as witches were said to be.

Known as the Night Riders, a band of men and women roamed the countryside on horseback. Hidden behind cloaks and gruesome masks, they struck fear into the hearts of those who chanced to come upon them.

They came one night to a shepherd's cottage standing alone on the shoulder of a hill. The inhabitants peered through the window as the sound of galloping hoofs drew near like the approach of thunder. Then, along the moonlit path, the Night Riders appeared.

The shutters were fastened, and the lamp turned low. While his wife and daughter stood trembling in a corner of the room, the shepherd grasped the heavy stick with which he sometimes drove wolves from the fold.

The riders came close, and the shepherd heard voices calling to him. But he dared not venture outside. Around and around the horses galloped, their hoofs tearing the ground. And louder came the riders' calling. Then they lit torches and threw them upon the timbers of the roof. Soon the room burst into flames, and the inhabitants were forced to unbolt the door and stumble outside, choking and fighting for breath. The raiders swept upon them, their mocking laughter drowning cries of alarm.

It seemed a long time before the sound of the horses' hoofs was heard fading away.

The shepherd's smoke-filled eyes were burning. Beside him lay his wife, dazed and trembling with fright. The gates of the fold were open, and sheep ran bleating over the hillside. But although they searched the smouldering cottage and called repeatedly into the darkness, their daughter was never found.

In time the cottage was rebuilt. Lambs from the fold were lost forever, carried away for sacrificial slaughter. And one day, as though in answer to their prayers, the girl wandered home again.

All summer long she would only sit and stare, unable – or too afraid – to explain what had happened to her: as though she had found some darkness where her tortured mind had crawled for refuge.

✽   ✽   ✽

It was a winter evening when a villager from the lowlands was making his way home. There was no moon. The wind was whispering as snowflakes flurried about. He turned up his collar against the cold, quickening his step. 'Not far to go,' he murmured. 'Not far now. Past the church and over the hill . . .' Then he would see the lamplight glowing in the windows along the street. 'Not far now.'

The church was dark, its steeple lost in the sky. Beyond was the cemetery wall, stretching into the night. It was not until he came to the gate that he saw a light among the tombstones. It flickered in the far corner toward the marsh where fresh graves were dug.

The gate creaked as he pushed it open, barely wide enough to squeeze through. From there he felt his way along the trodden paths between the graves. Slowly, silently. Not a sound must betray his presence.

At first he imagined that a gravedigger was preparing someone's resting place. But as he approached, the light glowed brighter, and he heard a murmuring – voices swelling and fading, like the chanting of prayers. Once his heart raced when ivy tangled at his feet and held him fast.

Closer now, he could see the silhouettes of a hooded group gathered around an open grave. Swathed in cloaks, their bodies merged with the darkness. The death masks that hid their faces showed in the glow of torchlight, grey as that of the corpse they had disturbed from its resting place.

Voices uttered strange invocations. But he dare not venture nearer, for he suspected that he had come upon a band of Night Riders engrossed in some profane ceremony – consorting with the spirit of the departed, descending into Hades to keep company with the Devil.

He knew that if he waited longer he would see the corpse staked up to stand among them, watch them scratch their voodoo circle in the earth. When the ceremony was over they would move like shadows to their horses tethered nearby, leaving only the mouldering remains to wait for the dawn.

But he had lingered there long enough. He moved away, his footsteps as quiet as the falling snowflakes, retracing a path among the mounds and epitaphs, through the rusty gate. He would mention nothing of what he had seen. He would guard the secret well, sharing it with no one, for it was well-known that the vengeance of the Night Riders was swift and fearful.

Demons of Loudun

Long ago the nuns at a convent in Loudun, south of the Loire, told of their chapel and cloisters being bewitched by demons. Whenever they were at prayer icy draughts rustled their habits, and an animal cry, like that of a howling wolf, echoed from the rafters.

Mysteriously, timbers and masonry became dislodged and fell on them. More than once, inhabitants of the convent were stricken with a strange infirmity, for a time their heads and limbs convulsing, and then their bodies becoming rigid so that they could only stare into the shadows. It was the prayers of their sisters that drove away the sickness.

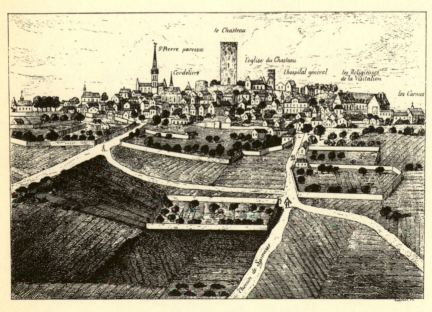

A view of Loudun in the 17th century.

ÆT. 37.
1627.

Father Urbain Grandier.

The execution of Father Urbain Grandier, 1634.

Suspicion fell on a Father Urbain Grandier, for it was whispered that he had forsaken his vows and had taken for his mistress a young girl who had come to him for confession.

'He has two demons to obey his commands,' the girl confessed. 'They are called Asmodeus and Zabulon.' And pity help those whom the devils possessed, she led her examiners to believe. She told how Grandier's incubi, his attendant demons, came to her in nightmares, forever waking her from sleep so that she was heavy-eyed and exhausted.

The parish priest's trial in 1633 attracted much interest. From the outset he protested his innocence, not relenting even under torture. But the evidence against him was overwhelming. Witch marks were found on his body, and a covenant was found between him and the Devil, written in Latin and signed with blood. There were many who bore witness to his sacrilege.

It is recorded that after his conviction he was tied to a ladder, hoisted above the crowds, and then slowly lowered into a bonfire by his executioners. His judge, meanwhile, stood by to ensure that his punishment was carried out as prescribed by the law.

It is believed that the evil which possessed Father Urbain Grandier did not perish with him in the flames, and that vengeance reached out from beyond the grave. Long after his ashes had smouldered, certain of his accusers met with tragic ends, and the nuns of the convent at Loudun continued to suffer convulsive fits from time to time, and some were known to stare, wild-eyed and mutter 'Asmodeus' or 'Zabulon'.

The Witchdoctor

With the advance of education and science, belief in the paranormal faded during the eighteenth century. In the Western world witchcraft laws were repealed, and fear of the unknown became tempered with understanding. But in the far corners of civilization, where tribal customs prevail, an obsession with the wonders of witchery and the black arts lives on.

In parts of Africa, even during recent years, gruesome evidence has come to light of chilling rituals performed by the *inyangas* – the tribal witchdoctors whose magic and *muti* is held to be a gift from the gods.

Reports tell of a young boy whose brain had been pierced with nails, and of *Muti-men* who cut out the tongue of a child and severed the hand of another, because they believe that when parts of human bodies are scattered in the fields the soil becomes more fertile. Likewise, when they are stuffed into medicinal horns magical powers are enhanced. The head of a corpse, stolen from a funeral parlour, was buried beneath the earthen floor of a kraal so that the inhabitants should be blessed with good fortune.

It is the witchdoctor who perpetuates these age-old superstitions. In tribal communities he is revered above all others. It is he who, by black magic, can stir peaceful villagers into a bloodthirsty mob.

The village of Seruleng lies hidden in the red dust of the Northern Transvaal, a full day's trek from Zebediela. Steeped in tribal tradition, it is a place where goats wander freely on the dirt roads, and where children flee to their mother's arms at the approach of a fair-skinned visitor.

Not long ago a young woman of the village died mysteriously the day after attending the wake of a relative. Distressed at their

194

ΛPIRE
•BOOKS•

Phone Orders
Gladly Accepted!

CENTRE TOWN
240 Bank (at Lisgar)
236-2363

**LINCOLN HEIGHTS
GALLERIA**
2525 Carling Avenue
820-7023

sister's suffering and sudden death, her brothers sought the counsel of the witchdoctor.

That night spells were chanted to invoke the ancestral spirits, and ceremonial bones were scattered on the ground. The witchdoctor's eyes shone bright in the firelight.

**Ceremonial bones scattered
on the ground by a Kaffir witch doctor in Africa.**

Presently the drums were silent and the chanting ceased. At the funeral wake the young woman's food was poisoned, the spirits had whispered. And the bones spelled out that another *inyanga* was the culprit.

Roused to anger, the family and friends of the victim seized the murderer and dragged him off to the bush. There he was hacked with knives and beaten mercilessly while others gathered wood to build a pyre on which he was to burn.

In terror the *inyanga* fought to escape, protesting that he was not alone in the wicked plot. He swore that two women of the tribe had bribed him to prepare a poisonous draught for them to administer at the wake. The victim, he explained, had stolen their husband's affection and he had forsaken them.

With no evidence, other than the *inyanga's* accusation, to

implicate the jealous women, they too were snatched away in the night.

Far from the village, the *inyanga* and his alleged accomplices were bound together while kindling was gathered and set alight. As the flames licked higher their screams rang out over the veldt. A band of villagers chanted and jeered as the fire engulfed them.

Tribal custom and justice had run its course, for it is believed that only fire will drive away evil spirits. The following morning all that remained were charred bones among the ashes.

The girl sat in the shade of the trees that lined the city street. People passed by with hardly a glance at a lowly hawker.

'Fresh, sweet oranges,' she called after them. 'Very cheap.' She pointed to her basket, heaped with fruit, golden as the sunshine.

But no one stopped to buy. Everyone hurried along, for they had seen the dark clouds gathering on the horizon and had heard a rumbling above the drone of traffic.

Before long the daylight turned to dusk as the storm approached. The girl remembered the first heavy raindrops rustling the leaves overhead; a confusion of people running for shelter; a streak of light tearing the sky; the sudden crack of thunder. Then came a blinding flash after which she had the sensation of falling faster and farther into a deep pit of darkness.

She had no recollection of being taken to her home. Now it was evening and her family were gathered around her bed, wiping her forehead and tending her injuries.

'Thabo . . . Thabo . . .' Over and over she muttered the name of a young man from the village who had long tried in vain to win her affection and take her for his wife. She looked fearfully into the darkened corners of the room, as though someone were hiding there.

Her thoughts wandered, and she told of a bolt of lightning striking fire into a tree under which she had stood, recalling that moments before it struck, a black cat had appeared, brushing against her legs. This was a sure sign that the lightning had been sent by evil spirits to harm her.

Thabo – he was the malevolent one. It was he who had released the black magic, in vengeance for his unrequited love.

No one disputed that what the girl had suspected was true. At the time the young man had been far away working in the fields. He had conjured no spirits, nor harboured any grievance towards the girl. But no one could believe that it was the hand of fate that struck – a chance stroke of misfortune.

The family wanted just retribution. But the victim held a tender spot in her heart for the young man, and thought that smoke and flames was too fearful a penalty. Instead, she wished that he might go mad and forget about her.

But it was the *inyanga* who would decide. If it were Thabo whom the bones of the ancestral spirits described then the fire must be lit, for that was the way of their tribal laws, a tradition which could never be changed.

* * *

The Aborigines were the first inhabitants of Australia. Their origin is obscure, but it is believed that they crossed a land bridge to the north of the continent – a bridge which existed in prehistoric times.

A race of nomadic hunters, travelling in family groups or clans, there were some 300,000 Aborigines living in Australia when British settlers arrived at the end of the eighteenth century. But in conflicts with the settlers their numbers were severely depleted, and today the majority are confined to reserves in the desert and coastal regions of northern and central Australia. Some have chosen to work as stockmen on cattle and sheep stations, abandoning their natural way of life.

The habits of the more primitive of the Aborigines are simple. Ignorant of agriculture, the women of the clans continue to forage for plants and roots which are grubbed from the soil with a pointed stick. The men are skilled trackers and hunters, using only crude weapons such as spears, flint-tipped arrows, stone knives and fire-hardened boomerangs.

Like the natives of Africa, they have preserved age-old beliefs and customs. They wear little or no clothing, yet survive the intense heat of day and the bitterly cold night of the desert. Forever wandering in search of food, they build flimsy shelters and lie at night close to their fires of brushwood.

At certain times families gather as tribes to perform strange ceremonies concerned with hunting and the initiation of youths into manhood.

Not long ago a boy of the Northern Territory strayed from his home and was wandering in the outback. Daylight swiftly changed to darkness, hiding the landmarks which might guide him. Uncertain of his whereabouts, he led his horse through the shrubs and woodland, searching for the river bank which would point his direction home. But he could hear no sound of murmuring water, only the night birds calling.

Presently he heard a moaning sound in the distance, like the wind whispering through the bushes. And a glow appeared, flickering among the trees. As he approached he could distinguish voices chanting and silhouettes moving around a fire. He dismounted and crept closer, until he could see a band of Aborigines engrossed in some ritual dance. Their naked bodies glistened in the firelight, and their witchdoctor was painted all over in an intricate design, with strings of bones hanging about his neck and forehead.

The intruder had come upon a sacred ceremony, performed to mourn the death of a chief. This was their recitation of tribal lore, accompanied by the dance of *corroboree* – a jealously guarded ritual.

A witchdoctor is known to summon fearful magic. His curses send victims into a trance from which they seldom recover. As the boy watched from the seclusion of the trees, his horse whinneyed restively. Abruptly the ceremony ceased and the dancers were still. They searched around until the intruder was found and seized by angry clansmen. Trembling, the boy now stood before the witchdoctor, held at the mercy of his magic.

No one knows what happened to him that night. The next day he was found lying in the outback. He was breathing with difficulty and barely alive. It was thought that he had fallen from his horse, although he showed no sign of injury. His face was like a death mask, and nothing his rescuers did could rouse him from his trance. Throughout that day he stared fixedly, as though some power held him spellbound.

When, at length, the spell wore away and the boy recovered, he was afraid to be left alone. And for a long time he was haunted by the voice of a witchdoctor chanting a mysterious curse.

*   *   *

Among the more primitive of African tribes macabre beliefs in witchcraft still thrive. Along the Nile–Congo divide, the Azande believe that the powers to charm and weave spells are held within the hearts of the chosen ones and are passed from one generation to the next. Witches, they say, are able to fly through the night sky, emitting light like a falling star. They steal the souls of their victims who gradually waste away.

The tribes of the Bechuan and Basuto tell of the *baloi* who gather at night to dance naked and plunder the graves of those recently interred. They eat the corpse's flesh, believing that in so doing they capture a spirit that has not travelled far on its journey to the Otherworld. By practising this gruesome ritual the magic of the *baloi* is enhanced and their spells become more fearful.

The Lovedu of the Transvaal describe the *vuloi* whose spells make women barren, wither crops, and have owls and hyenas as their familiars.

Other tribal witches are said to glow like fireflies; to send out their 'shadow-soul' while the body sleeps. These phantom spirits gather on the branches of the baobab tree, to prey on their victims like vampires.

Those who fear and suffer have only the witchdoctor to defend them. He is the soothsayer, the diviner, whose mysterious medicine and magic ward off the evil spirits.

The night birds cried out and the drum-beat sounded beyond the village, waking the Azande witches from their sleep. One by one they stole from their beds, for this was the witch's call, summoning them to a secret rendezvous at a clearing in the jungle.

There their evil plot was hatched. Their victim was chosen with cunning – someone from the village, alone and in a deep sleep after an evening's feasting and drinking. Now his body lay slumped on the ground, and like ghouls they danced about him, their eyes glinting with expectation.

At their rendezvous a ritual murder was performed, to feed their powers while the victim's spirit still lived within him. One can readily imagine the agony he suffered as their devilish brew simmered over a fire. Flesh and eyes, lips and tongue, all were cut away. Burning stones stemmed the flow of blood, for while the heart was beating the longer the spirit lived.

An hour passed before death brought an end to suffering, and the Azande witches tasted the ghastly brew. The mutilated corpse was buried in a shallow grave, while far away the villagers still slept.

Until the moon grew full and bright again the horror continued. At nightfall the drums would sound, witches would steal away, and when morning came one of the tribe was never to return. Others were tormented by fearful dreams from which they woke delirious. The village was bewitched, and fear spread like a jungle fire.

It was the witchdoctor who was to rid them of the curse.

In the moonlight a circle was marked out with white ashes and horns stuck in the ground. No one but he was allowed to enter the circle lest the spell would be broken. Around the edges stood a band of drummers and a chorus of boys who began a ritual chant.

When the fire was burning fiercely the witchdoctor leapt among them, arrayed in his traditional regalia – a head-dress decked with feathers; a loin cloth of animal skin; belt, bracelet and anklets of plaited reeds on which hung bones, teeth and claws from the carcasses of wild beasts. Around his neck he wore a chain of magic whistles made from bamboo boughs. His face and limbs were streaked with dye, and he moved towards the circle like a writhing snake.

The drums began a rhythmic beat. The chanting voices swelled. The witchdoctor danced at the centre, slowly at first, then, as the tempo was raised, more furiously, whipping himself into a frenzy and slashing his arms and chest with a knife until blood flowed freely and spilled on the ground.

'Who among us are the evil ones?' his voice cried out. 'Good spirits, point them out!'

As the fury of his dance slowed down, voices called out from those who mourned their lost ones, and those still under a spell. They offered a reward of coins and cattle if he could point out the witches and break the curse that had fallen upon the village.

Witch doctors appealing for rain.

The witchdoctor blew several tones on his whistles to invoke ancestral spirits. Then he stared into a pot of water into which raindrops had fallen, searching for the reflection of the evil ones. He called out into the night, and then listened intently as though faraway voices were calling back.

The witches, who were there among the villagers, looked about furtively as the witchdoctor searched for images in his magic pot and listened for an answer from the spirit world. Afraid that they might be discovered, they backed away toward the trees.

'See how they creep away!' cried one of the villagers.

'The evil ones!' the witchdoctor called after them.

Cries of anger grew, and the chase began. In terror the culprits fled, but there was no escape. Screaming, they were dragged back to the clearing where they were to await their sentence.

The fire smouldered on until the first light of dawn. The witches had perished in its flames and their ashes were scattered to the four winds.

It was believed that the souls of their victims had now been restored, to live on in the ancestral resting place. Others who were bewitched and plagued with nightmares were placed under the care of the witchdoctor until the sparkle came back to their eyes and they slept peacefully through the night.

*   *   *

A newspaper of thirty years ago records an unusual story of witchcraft.

In 1957 a new pupil arrived at a native school situated in Uganda where the hills sloped gently down to the valley of the Nile.

Much of her time was spent alone, tending her father's sheep beyond the village to the south. At school no one chose her as a friend. Whenever the children were at play she stood aside and watched, and was never invited to join in the fun. Sometimes she was teased by other girls. 'All alone . . . all alone . . . Little Miss All Alone,' they would chant when they saw her standing in the corner of the playground. Then they would laugh and taunt until her eyes filled with tears.

The strange incident began one day when the children were playing their favourite game. While one girl covered her eyes and counted to a hundred the others ran to hide among the bushes or behind the trunks of trees that surrounded the school. But on this occasion, while each was crouched in a chosen hiding place, the seeker grew tired of the game and wandered off.

Unknown to those who hid, it was Little Miss All Alone who set out in search of them, a mischievous smile on her lips.

First she searched among the shrubs where she had seen the foliage stir and heard stifled voices giggling. Quietly she crept into the dusky light beneath the leaves. There was no gasp of surprise: no cry of excitement. The girls hiding there were struck speechless with fright. It was not the seeker whom they saw peeping in at them. Their eyes were fixed on a snake that came slithering along the ground towards them.

Next, Little Miss All Alone peered through the window of the gardener's shed, where more of the children were hiding behind the door. When she pushed it open no one recognized the seeker standing in the doorway. There were screams of terror, for there they saw a beast with burning eyes and bared teeth.

Along the perimeter she continued her search, hidden in the shade of the trees. 'I'm coming to find you . . . to find you!' they heard a deep voice call.

Farther and farther the pursuer prowled, while the fugitives were too afraid to utter a sound. Could it be the cloven hoofs of the Devil that were seen imprinted on the ground?

Some children had climbed among the lower branches of a tree. Now they were staring down, their eyes wide with fear, as the tree caught alight and flames spread from bough to bough.

For many days the mystery remained, and the children were afraid to venture into the playground. They told of unearthly sounds, and imagined that the school on the hillside had fallen under a spell.

It was only the lonely girl who knew the secret.

After studying his scattered bones and enchanted pool of reflections, the witchdoctor discovered that the new girl was the daughter of a witch, whose power had passed to the next generation. Their home in the village was searched, and hidden in a chest were found a human skull, the withered paw of a monkey and other grisly charms of witchery and black magic.

For practising witchcraft, which was forbidden by state laws, the woman was sent to gaol. And for her mischief Little Miss All Alone was caned and made to promise that never again would she dabble in her mother's black arts.

Bibliography

The following is a list of publications consulted during the preparation of this collection. There were, in addition, stories from old newspapers and magazines rescued from obscurity by County Archivists and local historians throughout the United Kingdom and abroad.

S.O. Addy, *Folktales and Superstitions* (Wakefield, Yorkshire, 1973)

H. Bloom, *Folklore and Superstitions in Shakespeare's Land* (Michell & Clark, London, 1921)

W. Brockie, *Legends and Superstitions of Durham* (Wakefield, Yorkshire, 1974)

J.A. Brooks, *Ghosts and Witches of the Cotswolds* (Norwich, 1981)

A. Dickinson, *Salem Witchcraft Delusion* (New York, 1974)

P. Haining, *Witchcraft and Black Magic* (London, 1971)

W. Henderson, *Folklore of the Northern Counties* (London, 1866; New Edition, London, 1879)

E. Jong, *Witches* (New York, 1981)

J. Kramer, H. Sprenger, *Malleus Maleficarum* (Italy, 1486)

T. Otway, *The Orphan or Unhappy Marriage* (University of Nebraska, 1976)

G. Parrinder, *Witchcraft – European and African* (London, 1973)

K. Radford, *Tales of South Wales* (Skilton & Shaw, London, 1979)

K. Radford, *Tales of North Wales* (Skilton & Shaw, London, 1982)

Readers Digest Association Limited, *Folklore Myths and Legends of Britain* (London, 1977)

R.H. Robbins, *The Encyclopedia of Witchcraft and Demonology* (London, 1959)

R. Seth, *In the Name of the Devil/Great Scottish Witchcraft Cases* (London, 1969; New York, 1970)

R. Scott, *Discoverie of Witchcraft* (Originally published 1584; reprinted Arundel, West Sussex, 1964)

Illustration acknowledgements

Mary Evans Picture Library, London: 56, 66, 82, 141, 173, 177, 183, 190, 191, 195

Fortean Picture Library, Corwen, Clwyd: 3, 15, 18, 40, 44, 69, 78, 111 (right), 121, 125, 182, 186

The Fotomas Index, London: 53, 111 (left), 192, 201

Macdonald/Aldus Archive, London: 10, 12, 25, 28, 31, 46, 80, 91, 103, 106, 115

The Mansell Collection, London: 60, 63, 74, 97, 128

Peter Newark's Historical Pictures, Bath: 20, 22, 36, 102, 132, 154, 180